MOEEN

MOEEN

MOEEN ALI

with Mihir Bose

ALLEN&UNWIN

First published in Great Britain in 2018 by Allen & Unwin
Copyright © 2018 by Moeen Ali

The extract from DNA India on pp. 200–202 is reproduced with the
kind permission of Arunabha Sengupta.

Allen & Unwin
c/o Atlantic Books
Ormond House
26–27 Boswell Street
London WC1N 3JZ

Phone: 020 7269 1610
Fax: 020 7430 0916
Email: UK@allenandunwin.com
Web: www.allenandunwin.com/uk

A CIP catalogue record for this book is available from the British Library.

All images in the photo insert, unless otherwise credited, are © Moeen Ali.

Hardback ISBN 978 1 91163 005 0
Trade paperback ISBN 978 1 91163 013 5
E-Book ISBN 978 1 76063 549 7

CONTENTS

PROLOGUE

THE MAGIC OF THE OVAL

As every fan knows, sport can be gloriously unpredictable – and cricket is no exception. Players, fans and media experts alike are sometimes totally unprepared for a surprise outcome. One such event was when a 'part-time bowler' became the first England spinner to take a Test match hat-trick for 79 years, on a ground staging its hundredth Test where no hat-trick has ever been taken. I still find it hard to believe that I was that bowler at the Oval when on the afternoon of 31 July 2017, just before 2.30, I got the South African number eleven, the fast bowler Morne Morkel, lbw. Nobody anticipated that I would make history, especially when you consider that there were two England bowlers who had had the opportunity to write themselves into the record books in that innings before I got Morkel. Both Ben Stokes and Toby Roland-Jones had taken two wickets in two balls in that South African second innings, Stokesy, the previous evening and Toby that very morning in the pre-lunch session. Now as Morkel was given out I felt like the man seen as a defensive midfield anchor scoring a hat-trick to win the FA Cup. And this when the forwards had not quite managed it. To make it even more special I had never taken a

3

hat-trick in any form of cricket before, not even when I played for Moseley Ashfield as a teenager in Birmingham.

Before that magical moment at the Oval I had had much to celebrate on a cricket field: hundreds, five wickets in an innings, wins and even two wickets in two balls. But a hat-trick had eluded me and until you've actually had one you cannot imagine what a hat-trick feels like. My hat-trick also meant England won the Test, giving us a 2-1 lead with one Test to go which meant we could not lose the series and as the England team hoisted me on their shoulders I had the most amazing feeling I've had on a cricket pitch. I've never had that feeling. I'll never experience it again.

But although I had never imagined I would take a hat-trick in the series against South Africa, I was through that summer often doing things that had not happened for a long time. At Lord's in the first Test I had taken 6 for 53 in the second innings, giving me match figures of 10 for 112. Those were not only my career-best figures in both innings, it was the first time an England spinner had taken ten wickets in a Lord's Test since the legendary Derek Underwood against Pakistan in 1974. At Lord's I had also made runs: 87 in the first innings, putting on 257 for the fifth wicket with skipper Joe Root who made a quite brilliant 190. This meant I had reached a nice Test all-rounder's landmark of 2,000 runs and 100 wickets, the second-fastest for England since Tony Greig. I'd always hoped I'd get onto the board at Lord's as a batsman but never thought I'd be there as a bowler – it was something I didn't expect but I'm very proud of.

As I left Lord's with the Man of the Match award the *Guardian* wrote, 'Moeen leads the team off, his body language as modest as ever. He is a pretty adorable bloke, and a fine cricketer who has finally found the perfect role in this side.' Trevor Bayliss, the England coach, had put a bit of a dampener on things, saying after Lord's, 'We selected him as a batter who bowls a bit. Maybe that has taken the pressure off.' Yet through that summer I had felt no pressure as a bowler and at Trent Bridge in the second Test my 4 for 78 in the second innings were the best figures for an England off-spinner since 1956. So, I arrived in SE11 feeling quite confident. Before the start of the Test I remember thinking this could be a series where I could be consistent with both bat and ball and make contributions to help the team win. True, we had come to the Oval branded by the media as the Jekyll and Hyde team. At Lord's in the first Test we had crushed South Africa by 211 runs with a day to spare in Rooty's first Test as captain. Set 331 to win, South Africa had begun their second innings after lunch but were bowled out for 119 by the close, their innings lasting just 36.4 overs. Eight days later in the second Test at Trent Bridge South Africa won by 340 runs. Chasing 474, we were bowled out for 133, our second-innings capitulation coming in less than two sessions. Anyone who has played sport at a high level knows that results are everything: you are either a huge success or a major failure. There is no halfway house. Succeed and the critics will praise you to the skies, fail and they cannot wait to bury you. After Trent Bridge critics were immediately on our back, saying they never knew which England will turn up at Tests. Would it be Dr Jekyll or Mr Hyde? This inconsistency was meat and drink to the to the former players turned pundits.

Geoffrey Boycott called our batting one-dimensional. Nasser Hussain said, 'A positive brand is not 130 all out, that's a rubbish brand of cricket.' And he definitely had a point. In the warm weather at Trent Bridge Scyld Berry of the *Telegraph* compared our performance with ice cream: 'on an afternoon of gorgeous heat,' he wrote, 'England's batting melted away by three o'clock. They were bowled out in fewer than 50 overs as South Africa won the second Test ... even more resoundingly than England had won the first.' I was not spared, and, in a week, I went from being 'a pretty adorable bloke' to an English ice cream that melted at the first sight of the sun. The television commentators charged me with 'throwing my wicket away' when I was caught sweeping at square-leg in the second innings.

But despite such media criticism I and the team as a whole came to the Oval feeling far from depressed. Indeed, quite confident we could beat South Africa. You only had to see us play football in the days leading up to the Test, and even on the morning of the match, to realize how high our spirits were. The days of the double internationals have long gone – the nature of modern sport means they will never return – but the passion we have for the round-ball game has often made me think that in another age many of the present team would not look out of place at Wembley. I certainly would have loved, come September, to change from the whites to shorts and make the brief journey from Lord's to Wembley to once again perform for England. I love football, am besotted with Liverpool and nothing would have given me greater pleasure than to run out at Wembley wearing the number nine jersey. I grew up wanting to be another Robbie Fowler. Now I fancy myself as Luis Suárez, although in the 2017–18 season I have also seen myself as Mohamed Salah. But then which Red fan has not? With the Uruguayan Suárez having used not only his feet but also his teeth I occasionally get teased, but I have never bared my fangs, not even when I am tackled by Stuart Broad, who sees himself as the defender you cannot get past. I must say our football has at times been so intense that matches have had to be stopped. To prevent injury, we play three-touch football but Jimmy Anderson and Jos Buttler, our midfield dynamos, can get so ferocious that Paul Farbrace, our assistant coach who organizes our football, often has to intervene. He has even had to stop games. Then Jimmy starts moaning so loudly about biased refereeing that I feel we could do with FIFA's Video Assistant Referee system.

We play seven-, eight- or nine-a side football with the management always in goal. Teams are selected for a series and the best part is when it comes to choosing a side. You should see the look on Ben Stokes's face. You cannot imagine an England cricket team without Stokesy, but he's always the last to get picked. Unlike me and the others he is not a fanatical football man, he sort of supports Newcastle and when it comes to football he is the butt of most of the jokes. Yes, we say, you know how to kick a ball, but you cannot read a game, you do not have a clue. Stokesy does not take kindly to such ripping.

But that is all part of the fun and it helps with getting the guys going. Some days you're going to wake up maybe a little bit more tired, lethargic or whatever. With the matches always played in the morning it peps you up and, in the run-up to a Test, it is a big thing and the most important part of the day. It's something everybody enjoys. It also provides the dressing room banter that can be so helpful in bonding us together, even more so after a defeat with the media baying for our blood. It also brings out our eccentricities, which only adds to the fun. Broady, a Forest supporter, gets very upset if we call his team by that name. 'It is Nottingham Forest Football Club' he will say loudly and glare at us with the same fiercely disdainful look he will give a batsman who has just played and missed.

Paul Farbrace, the equivalent of Gareth Southgate when it comes to football, is a fanatical Chelsea supporter and I love ripping him. I also love getting stuck into our batting coach Mark Ramprakash, who in the great tradition of Middlesex players supports the red side of north London. In the last two years Ramps has not much enjoyed me asking him when Arsène Wenger will be given the push and contrasting the fortunes of the Arsenal manager with how well Jürgen Klopp is making Liverpool great again. We do have to put up with endless bragging from Jose (aka Jos Buttler), who is in love with Manchester City. But it is easier to deal with Chris Woakes, a fanatical Aston Villa supporter, and Jimmy Anderson, who loves Burnley to bits. They do not have much to talk about and the conversation about the deeds of their football teams can be short and for me rather sweet, although as the 2017–18 season progressed Jimmy did perk up.

The lead-up to the Oval Test was no different with Jimmy getting upset when Farby, as we call Paul Farbrace, stopped the game because of his tackling, Stokesy getting furious when we kept saying he is not made for football and Rooty, who supports Sheffield United and fancies himself as a striker, finding that I was bulging the net more often than he ever could. But then at the risk of sounding a braggart I am sure since we've been playing football I hold the Golden Boot. It was after I had banged in yet another goal in our warm-up match that I had a look at the Oval wicket the Surrey groundsman had prepared and thought it would have to suddenly change in character if my wickets tally were to match the number of goals I was scoring.

The wicket did not look as it would provide much help for spin. That is hardly surprising. We had come to the Oval a month earlier than normal, end of July rather than end of August. For much of the match there was little to make me feel I had misread the wicket. The start, of course, given our batting at Trent Bridge, was a bit anxious. But then Alastair Cook, not a great football fan – he supports Luton – and a wonderful century by Stokesy meant the Trent Bridge debacle was soon a distant memory. To finish with 353 was a good effort and that total looked even better when Toby Roland-Jones, or Rojo to his teammates, made the sort of debut we all dream about. The

Middlesex bowler took five wickets in his first innings, bowling South Africa out for 175. I had little to do, bowling just 5 overs. We started batting in the second innings with a lead of 178, and with the boys not throwing away the advantage we had, I had even less to do. I didn't even watch much of our batting. I try to watch a game as much as I can but the hardest days in Test cricket for me are the days when we win the toss, we're batting first, and I have nothing to do. I have the biggest headache after the game if I just keep watching. I find it mentally tough and get fatigued.

To make it worse there is a huge problem when we develop a partnership because of the rule Cooky imposes in the dressing room. If we are sitting in a particular order when the partnership has begun, we cannot move. You've got to sit where you were sitting when the partnership started. If you want to move, you must leave the dressing room. I do get up and go to the toilet and say to Cooky, 'Look, I don't believe in that. If he gets out he gets out.' But Cooky is big on this sort of thing and he will say, 'No, you must stay there, and everyone's got to stay in the same position.' If the partnership is still going on then even when you go off for tea or have a drinks interval you must come back to the position you were in before the break.

So, in the second innings with the guys playing well I decided to leave the dressing room altogether and went with Saqlain Mushtaq, our spin-bowling coach, downstairs to the indoor nets at the Oval. There, while Stokesy carried on as he had in the first innings I bowled for a very long time with Saqlain.

These days sport has become so computerized that you get all sorts of graphics and data analysing everything happening on the field of play. You get stats that were just not available when I first started playing cricket. Some players like it, but to be honest I'm not a massive fan. I don't doubt that it has its uses but it's not for me. Probably half the England team like to look at those stats with Dawid Malan, Alastair Cook and Joe Root very fond of turning to the computer to see how they've done. Stats have even come into spin bowling in a big way. Commentators make much of the speed with which the ball is delivered or how many revolutions a spinner gives to the ball. I'm not bothered about checking such stats. This may make me old-fashioned but as I see it, regardless of the revolutions, if the shape of the ball is not right it might not spin.

Instead of machines I prefer to talk to humans and there is no one better to talk to than Saqlain. He is my spin guru, one of the great experts in off-spin bowling. He gets you to under-stand your own bowling. He provides the finest details you could ever imagine, opening what he calls 'doors' in bowling spin. No computer could do that. So, for example, he tells me, 'Try and hit a good area and bowl your best bowl all the time.' This does not mean I should bowl the doosra. That is not the advice he gives me. Just to bowl orthodox off-spin and try and hit the top of the stumps. That afternoon at the indoor nets at the Oval Saqlain kept talking to me, encouraging me by point-ing out that through the summer things were getting better with my bowling.

As I practised in the underground nets at the Oval the words running through my head were my father's: that hard work pays off and you see the rewards for working hard. I might not see the rewards now. I've just got to keep working hard, stay on top of my bowling. My efforts will pay off. What encouraged me further was that in contrast to previous seasons, where I had concentrated on my batting, I had never worked as hard on my bowling as I was now doing.

But as the fourth day's play ended it seemed I would not have much to do. We had declared at 313 for 8, setting South Africa 492 to win, and at one stage they were 52 for 4, with the media speculating the match might finish in four days. But led by Dean Elgar they had recovered to 117 for 4. The papers on the fifth morning certainly saw no role for me in what was seen as an easy England victory. Much of the speculation was whether Jimmy, who had celebrated his 35th birthday on the fourth day, would get a belated present from the South Africans on the final day.

For much of the pre-lunch session I had nothing much to do and if anybody looked like getting a hat-trick it was Rojo. He had Bavuma, the overnight not out, and Philander both lbw with successive balls. But while Morris edged the hat-trick ball it fell short of Stokesy so Rojo missed out.

With South Africa 168 for 6 and the clock showing that it was not yet twelve it looked like we would win. The only doubt was cast by Dean Elgar, the South African opener, who was batting well. Indeed he got to his hundred lofting me for 4 when on 97.

Then with only one over remaining before lunch Rooty brought me on. I was bowling to Morris, with whom I had had quite a few duels in the series. I remembered how he'd engineered to have me caught in Trent Bridge. The very first ball I bowled to him he edged but it hit Jonny 'Bluey' Bairstow on the knee. That was a near-impossible chance and Bluey would have to be very exceptional to take it. But it encouraged me that I could trap Morris. I decided that for the last ball before lunch I would try something Morris might not expect. I would not spin the ball and hope I could deceive him. That proved the case. Morris thinking it would spin played for the turn. It went straight and Stokesy, who makes every slip catch look so easy, took the catch with his customary style. He might not be able to read the moves in football but he anticipates slip catches in the way Mo Salah anticipates a defence-splitting pass and races forward to score.

As I watched Stokesy move to his left and take the catch I though how lucky I was to be playing with him. He's a massive inspiration. He is the best cricketer I've played with by a mile, one of England's great all-rounders, batting, bowling, fielding. He is also an amazing character to have around. He brings out the best in me on the pitch. This is both through how he encourages me with his advice and how he performs on the field. Sometimes he has said to me that he'll watch me play and he'll think, 'I need to play like that. Or, my mindset needs to be like that.' A lot of the time it's the other way around. I'll watch him play and think actually I need to be like him. That is exactly how I need to be today.

Stokesy for me is a massive player in terms of not just what he does on the field but in the dressing room. We could not be more different yet he is the best friend I have in the dressing room, a very kind, gentle guy who in private is different to his public persona. Stokesy is always coming up with ideas that bond the team together. So, during the South Africa series he had taken us go-kart racing. Although some of the players knew the sport – Jason Roy is quite brilliant at it – for me it was a new experience and without Stokesy I would never have thought of go-karting. Yes, he does have that other side where he's very competitive but he is also a very funny guy. He likes cracking jokes all the time.

But be warned: he doesn't take it kindly if you make jokes at his expense. So for example, if he's playing FIFA on the PlayStation or the Xbox, where I am Liverpool and he may be Real Madrid, and if I say, 'Ah, you know, Stokesy, you are the worst player' or something, he will just lose it, start shouting and even tell me to get out of the room.

This lunchtime as we trooped back to the pavilion I thought it would be a good idea if the team had a laugh at Stokesy's expense. I was ready with a joke. As we got back into the dressing room I said to the lads, 'You are in a box. There are no windows, no doors and you have to get out of the box. How do you get out? In one corner of the box you have a saw, in another you have a knife, in the third you have a gun and in the fourth you have a hen lay.' Stokesy, sitting in his favourite spot of the home dressing room at the Oval, had been listening to all this and suddenly said, 'A hen lay.' I replied, 'Yeah,' and he went, 'What's a hen lay?' I turned round to him and said, 'Eggs.' Everybody in the dressing room burst out laughing but Stokesy was stony faced. He just didn't get the joke and seeing his grim face we laughed even more. He didn't like it at all. Now you may think such banter at lunch of a Test you want to win sounds strange but in my view it is a great bonding experience. That lunchtime at the Oval was one of the funniest times I have experienced in an England dressing room and we came out for the afternoon session in great spirits.

However, the good humour didn't mean I had deluded myself about my performance. Despite getting Morris out I felt something was not quite right with my bowling. After lunch I bowled a spell but that did nothing to reassure me I was getting it right. Dean Elgar was batting well and there seemed no way I could get him out. There was only one thing to do. Speak to Saqlain. Half an hour after lunch, I went off and had a chat with Saqlain and as he always does he restored my confidence. He also suggested a plan to deal with Elgar.

I discussed the plan with Rooty. Elgar was still looking to drive and the plan was that I bowl wide to Elgar, get him to drive and this would trap him because I could get a bit more spin wide of the stump. The plan made perfect sense to me. The very first ball I bowled after my chat with Rooty floated outside the off-stump, Elgar obliged, went for a drive and as he edged the ball towards slip I knew he was out as Stokesy was there.

The next batsman in was Rabada. I'd had him caught at Lord's edging to Bluey but I had actually found him quite tough to bowl to throughout the series. He is quite a solid player and he can certainly hold a bat. Being a right-hander he also gave me a different angle. I decided I would follow the same plan that had worked for Elgar. As I ran in to bowl I thought let's see if Rabada goes for a big drive. So, I bowled almost exactly the same ball and got the same reward with Stokesy again taking the catch. South Africa were nine down. This wasn't the first time I'd taken two wickets in two balls, but I'd never managed a third in any form of the game and now it seemed the time had come to get that elusive hat-trick. Morne Morkel, the last man, had just walked in. Yet that was the last ball of the over. And Stokesy was going to bowl the next over. So with only one wicket to fall what chance did I have?

And this is where Stokesy's greatness as a human being and teammate came in. He had himself got two legs of a hat-trick the previous evening but failed to get the third. He was now bowling to Maharaj. When Stokesy started the over I did think he might get Maharaj out. I didn't mind him getting him out because it would mean we had won the match. After a couple of deliveries I was pretty sure he was deliberately bowling quite wide so that I could get my hat-trick. I was fielding at point at that time. After the third ball he looked at me and said, 'I'll make sure you bowl at Morne Morkel.' He ended up bowling three dot balls. After the fifth ball he looked at me and said, 'Don't worry, he will not get a single here. I'll make sure Morkel stays on strike for you.'

And for Stokesy to do that meant he would have to bowl wide so Maharaj could not play the ball. Maharaj is actually a good batsman. He's quite an aggressive kind of player, the sort who could reach and clout a wideish delivery. I must confess I was a bit anxious as Stokesy ran in to bowl those three balls, with all sorts of thoughts going through my head. Would Maharaj get a single and would I have to bowl to him? But Stokesy made sure it did not happen and I knew it was a great opportunity both for me to get my first hat-trick and for England to win the Test.

The break of an over before I bowled the hat-trick ball hadn't made me nervous. If anything, it helped me. What also helped was that once the umpire called over, Broady came up to me, stood right in front of me and said, 'You probably won't get a better opportunity of getting a hat-trick than bowling to a number eleven batsman. So be clear on what you're going to do and be convinced.' It was not only good advice but coming from a bowler who had taken two hat-tricks for England it was also very reassuring.

Morkel may be a number eleven but he is no mug with the bat. The days when the number eleven couldn't bat to save his life have long gone. In the first innings when I had bowled to Morkel he had taken guard on the leg-stump and played and missed a couple of balls. Then he decided to take guard on middle-and-off and suddenly he looked very comfortable. So much so that he had hit me through mid-wicket twice. But despite this I had thought I can get this guy out lbw if I bowl straight and he tries to hit me through the leg-side. However, in the first innings I never got the chance to bowl at him again.

Now as I saw him again take his guard on middle-and-leg I decided I would try to do what I couldn't in the first innings: tempt Morkel to drive through mid-wicket and get him lbw. As soon as I put the ball in my hand and turned to bowl the constant thought in my head was try and hit the stumps. That would give me the best chance. Maybe Morkel was expecting me to bowl another ball wide of the off-stump, a slower, spinning ball. And having hit me through mid-wicket in the first innings he probably felt comfortable. I don't know what went through his mind. As soon as the ball left my hand I knew the ball was going to be straight and when it hit Morkel's pads I knew he was out. As I spun round and appealed I expected Joel Wilson, the West Indian umpire, to raise his index finger. I couldn't believe it when he didn't do so. To this day I can't believe Wilson gave him not out. I looked at him with his arms by his side and thought, this cannot be not out. This has to be out. I can only speculate what went through his mind. I'd like to hope he was not overawed by the occasion. Maybe his heart wanted to give Morkel out but it was a big decision and he had to be absolutely sure and he was not. If that is the case I can understand it. Wilson was in a difficult situation for an umpire and didn't want it to be seen that he was wrong.

There was never any question that Rooty, who had been at mid-off, would review the decision. With nine down if there is any sort of chance you have to take it. In any case the team was almost unanimous Wilson had got it wrong. Bluey and Stokesy had the best view and as Bluey came up to me he said, 'Oh, that's really close.' Stokesy, typically, was even more emphatic, 'That's out.' By this time all the players were rushing in to huddle round me, Jimmy from gully, Keith Jennings from short-leg, Dawid 'Mal' Malan from leg slip, Cooky and Broady. They all echoed Stokesy and even started giving me the high fives. The unanimous support of my teammates further boosted my confidence that it could not be an umpire's call. That was the only thing that would save Morkel and deny me the hat-trick. And although as a bowler you can never be a hundred per cent sure this seemed unlikely. The decision was in the hands of the third umpire, Kumar Dharmasena, a man I knew well and who had given me a lot of bowling advice. I watched the screen as he scrutinized the television replays. However confident you are, a little shiver of fear does go through you as you watch the endless replays and you still need the three red lines to come up on the screen. I expected to see the three red lines but until they appeared I could not be sure. And when they did I felt such a surge of joy that I was a child again, jumping up and down on the pitch as the players hoisted me up. What put the icing on the cake was knowing that by getting Morkel's wicket we had won the match and now had a 2-1 lead in the series with one Test to go. We could not lose the series and might even win it. I knew what a big moment it was. Since the creation of the rainbow nation, and the resumption of England playing Test cricket against South Africa in 1994, we had won just one series at home against them and lost the last two. Defeats against the Proteas always seem to mean an England captain losing his job. Now there was no chance of that happening. And after being like ice creams melting in the hot sun only a week earlier, the victory felt very special.

What followed our win was in some ways the most touching moment of the Oval Test and one that made me feel, and always makes me feel, how much part of this England team I had become. To the onlooker the scenes after such a victory are the usual routine ones you see on any cricket field. A Test has been won, there is a group photograph with the winning team, somebody uncorks a bottle of champagne and it is sprayed all over the players. But because I don't drink or even touch alcohol I could not be part of any such scene. As we celebrated I could hear Cooky saying, 'Make sure Moeen gets in the picture first and then we can spray afterwards.' This is exactly what happened. I then walked away from the group photograph and my teammates were sprayed with champagne. The way the celebration was choreographed showed how much my teammates respected me as a person and also my culture and religion. It meant a massive amount to me. I cannot express how much I appreciated that and I felt this was a team I could give anything for.

For me the drink to celebrate with was a Coke and as I sipped one back in the pavilion it was wonderful to hear Saqlain, to whom I owe so much, saying, 'I just knew you were going to get it.' Even more wonderful was Hashim Amla coming to our dressing room and saying, 'As soon as you got two and Morkel was batting against you in that position I knew you were going to get the hat-trick.'

The boys were now back in the dressing room and as soon they all started singing *And so Sally can wait* from the Oasis song 'Don't Look Back in Anger', I knew it was time for me to go home. As the lyrics rang round an empty Oval I headed back to Birmingham. When I am driving I never listen to the cricket on the radio. Not even a single ball. I listen to lectures or talks on Islam, I listen to the Koran a lot in my car. I memorize it as much as I can. This is what I did that evening as I drove home. It makes me feel so wonderful. Wonderful as the hat-trick was, that means a lot more to me. I would later be told that while I listened to the Koran on the radio, on television and social networks the talk was all of what my hat-trick meant in the context of cricketing history. The Oval had been the home of Jim Laker, probably the greatest off-spinner in the history of the game, and Tony Lock, a marvellous left-arm-spinner – the pair that had been at the heart of Surrey's amazing seven championships in a row in the 1950s. But, noted the commentators, they had never taken a hat-trick for England at the Oval. And while the boys thought of Sally, many commentators were now convinced the hat-trick had taken me to a new level.

Before the hat-trick there'd been a lot of interest in the ethnic media and I won awards for ethnic sportsmen. Now it was the mainstream media that featured me. Less than a week after the Oval Test the *Guardian* devoted nearly two pages to an interview with me. Within two months I was proudly sporting my beard in the Saturday *Times* magazine. I look back on that media interest and think of my little boy growing up, playing cricket for England and me an old dad sitting in a stands watching him. And if he was a bowler I could be saying to the person sitting next to me, 'You know I got a hat-trick at a Test match.' I had done what every kid who ever bowls wants to and aspires to do as a youngster. Even to this day I sometimes have to really pinch myself and think, well, actually I have a Test hat-trick and no matter what happens from now on, no one can ever take that away from me. The hat-trick meant I felt I belonged, had come of age at last. It's what I had worked so hard all my life to do.

And what further thrilled me was the thought that the man who had done most to prepare me for this very special moment had witnessed it. That was my father. He had not been at the Oval but at home in Birmingham watching on television. Just before I left the Oval he and my mother had messaged me sounding very happy and proud. Soon after Donald McRae of the *Guardian*, who wrote the feature on me, had rung me and I had told him, 'I am sure he has watched every ball.' But when I finally arrived home I realized I was actually mistaken. Dad had actually not seen the hat-trick live, not been able to follow the drama of the most brilliant moment of my career. It was very sad but as he told the story to me I could not help laughing for there were some very funny moments in this curious tale.

My dad always gets nervous watching me play and I always say, 'I can understand you were nervous watching my first Test.

But there is nothing to be nervous about now.' The Test being in London was an additional problem for him. He has come to see me play in London but as he likes to drive, not take the train, parking is always a problem. He just about manages Lord's but the Oval is a nightmare. He can never find a parking space near the Oval. It is so bad that when he does venture into south London he has to take somebody with him to guide him around. So he decided he would watch the Oval Test on television. He was sitting comfortably in the sitting room of his house following the play on television when my wife Firuza, who was at the Oval, rang my mother to say that the gardener was coming to our house, could they go and let him in and also pay him. I was not bowling then, this was just after lunch when I had gone off the field to consult Saqlain, and Dad thought if we hurry we will be back in good time to see me bowl again. So Mum and Dad got in the car and nipped round to my house, a five-minute drive away.

Had they come straight home after that they would have seen me take the hat-trick but my mum said, 'Let's go to the bank, because it's nearly four o'clock now and it's going to shut.' Dad reluctantly agreed and it was while he was at the bank that his phone rang and it was a call from his cousin in Karachi. He seemed to say what sounded like 'Congratulations' but before my dad could speak and ask him what he was on about he got cut off. The cousin does not usually ring and Dad was worried something might have happened. He decided to go outside and the phone rang. It was his cousin again. This time the line was good and he heard, 'Mubarak, congratulations'. Not knowing why he was being congratulated, Dad said, 'What for? What's happened?' Now it was the turn of the cousin to be surprised. 'Where are you?' he asked, quickly adding, 'Moeen's taken a hat-trick!' So there standing outside a bank in Birmingham my dad learnt about my hat-trick at the Oval via a phone call from a cousin in faraway Karachi.

Dad rushed back inside the bank, pulled my mother out of the queue and said, 'We're going home.' He said to the cashier, by way of explanation, 'Moeen's taken a hat-trick.' The cashier stopped counting out money and shouted out, 'Moeen's taken a hat-trick.' Everyone in the bank now took up the cry. My dad, holding my mum's hand, ran out of the building, got in the car and drove straight home. As he sat watching replays of my hat-trick his phone would not stop ringing and he was flooded with text messages of congratulations. But he cannot hide his regret that he had missed witnessing my magical moment. That is a shame because without my dad and his great sacrifices, not only would I never have been in a position to take a hat-trick for England in a Test match, but I would never have got anywhere near playing cricket for England.

CHAPTER 1

WHO IS BETTY COX?

Just before the Ashes series of 2015 we went to a camp in Desert Springs in Andalucía in Spain. It is one of those classic sports camps that have developed in recent years, a sports complex in an isolated place. In winter it has ideal desert weather, warm and sunny. A lot of Premier League clubs use it for warm weather training, although unlike us they don't play cricket. Not surprising since many of their foreign players would not know what to make of the game. We did a lot of fielding and catching practice, cycling 14 kilometres to the beach, fitness work, golf for those who are fond of the game. And we played football all the time.

But while cricket has borrowed from football, our camp was not as regimented as the ones footballers have. We were treated more like adults and encouraged to think about what was best for us. In cricket the feeling then, and still is, you are grown-ups and it's your own career. Everyone's responsible for his own actions. If you mess up it's down to you. The view of the England management was, 'We are not nannies always monitoring what you are doing.' I agree with that approach. So, there was no curfew, nothing like that. And unlike footballers we weren't told what to eat. Arsène Wenger, the former Arsenal manager, may have revolutionized English football by bringing in special diets to increase the fitness of players. In cricket we have never had that sort of regime. We know we need the carbs to get through a day in the field and we have to stay fit but our food is nothing like as closely controlled as that of the footballer.

It was England coach Trevor Bayliss's first camp, an important moment and its real purpose was as a bonding exercise before the Ashes. As part of that we had to reveal facts about ourselves. One evening a quiz was organized. We had three quiz masters, Rooty was a matador, Stokesy was an Englishman abroad and Chris Taylor, our fielding coach, the Spanish golf legend Seve Ballesteros. Each of us had to give the quiz master a question which he read out to the rest of the squad. All sorts of questions were offered up by the various members of the team. My question was, 'My grandmother's name is Betty Cox. Who am I?' The quiz master read out the question and asked, 'Anybody know?' Everyone looked at each other and you could see they were completely stumped. It was obvious nobody had a clue. Eventually the quiz master asked, 'Nobody knows? Give up?' Everyone nodded. The format was that at this stage you had to put your hand up, get to your feet and reveal the answer. I stood up and nobody could believe it. I can still remember the look on director of cricket Andrew Strauss's face. He just could not believe it and still to this day can't believe that my grandmother's name is Betty Cox.

There are any number of England cricketers either born abroad, like Stokesy in New Zealand, or, like Straussy, born here but brought up in South Africa, but their names mean they are perceived to be English in the way I am not. In my case because of my name I am seen as a typical person of subcontinental origin who could not have any historic family connections with England. Most people cannot imagine that I've got an auntie called Ann who is my dad's half sister. I've got an uncle called Brett, Dad's half brother. All these relations, who could not be more English, are close family. My grandad treated Ann and Brett like his own children. My father is very close to Ann; she comes to my parents' home every week and Ann is as much my aunt as Shah Begum, my father's elder sister and Betty and Shafayat's first child. I grew up with Auntie Ann and Uncle Brett and still see them regularly. I realize when people look at me and think of my origins they would never think I have a family tree which is a bridge between England and Pakistan. At times I do feel boxed in. But the fact is my dad is half English, which makes me a quarter white.

I grew up hearing stories of how my grandfather Shafayat Ali met my grandmother Betty Cox. Nothing could be more romantic or a more wonderful insight into how after the Second World War this country took the first steps towards the multiracial, multicultural society we have now become. I have heard my grandparents' stories often and they always make me think how much we have changed and how far we have come as a nation.

Much is made of tales of mass migration and of people ending up far from the land of their birth, and when I consider my grandfather's life I realize that had things turned out differently I might have played for Australia. It was there Shafayat Ali headed when he first left the subcontinent just after the war. He was born in the small village of Dadyal in the district of Mirpur in Kashmir. Those were the days of the British Raj, although Kashmir was ruled by a maharaja, part of the third of the subcontinent which was ruled not by the British but by princes who had total internal autonomy and could do much as they liked in their own kingdom. In Kashmir this meant the maharaja invented a whole new way of playing cricket. Every time there was a cricket match he would arrive at three o'clock, the Kashmir national anthem would be played, salaams would be made and he would first retire to a special tent to smoke a long water pipe. At around 4.30, irrespective of which team was batting, he would come out to bat. Two attendants would pad him, one for each leg, two others put the gloves on, one for each hand. Then, while another attendant carried his bat, he sauntered to the middle, a small man wearing a large turban. Even if he was bowled he was given not out. Once the wicketkeeper called no-ball after the ball had hit the stumps. Eventually after fifteen or twenty minutes, by which time he had made 50, he would say he was tired and was given out lbw. The match carried on as if he had never been at the crease. History does not record what the scorer did with the 50 the maharaja had scored. How I would love to be given not out even when I am out!

But that was in the capital Srinagar. There was no cricket in Dadyal. My grandad didn't learn about the game until he came to this country and never took to it. His concern when leaving his little village was to get out and find work and this he did when he was sixteen or seventeen. He went first to Mumbai, one of the great cities of the British Raj, where he found work on a ship which took him to Australia. This was the era of the White Australia policy after the war, when the government, keen to get the British to migrate there, tried to attract the Ten Pound Poms. But they had to be white. It was not long after this that Harold Larwood, having terrorized Australian batting during the 1932 bodyline series and fed up with running a small shop in Blackpool, migrated to Australia under the Ten Pound Pom scheme. Many others – estimates say it was over a million and half – did the same. Who knows how my life would have turned out had Australia then allowed migrants from Asia. My grandad came back to Mumbai and from there sailed for England. He found work as a die-caster in the Lucas factory in Birmingham. It was at Lucas that he met Betty, a local girl from Acocks Green, and they married in 1949.

Betty's story is just as fascinating. Her first husband, a pilot, had died in the war and she was left to look after two young children, Ann and Brett. She knew little about the world my grandfather had come from. At that time in England there was little chance of knowing about it as there were very few Asians in this country. In a city as big as Birmingham there were only about ten people from Kashmir. My grandfather would often

31

tell the story of a guy called Zaman who had come from Kashmir a year or two before him. He was the first to arrive and was seen as some sort of pioneer.

Strangers, they say, do attract. I don't know whether it was that, but my grandparents' love for each other was deep and overcame all racial and cultural differences. In those days mixed marriages were unknown and there was overt racism in this country of the type we, thankfully, do not see today. My grandfather saw signs outside boarding houses saying, 'No dogs, Irish or coloured'. It helped that my grandmother's family accepted my grandad. From the beginning my grandmother took to her husband's culture and faith. She converted to Islam and when in 1956 he decided that their young children should go back to his village for their basic education, reading the Koran, saying Namaz, or prayers, she readily accepted.

I can only wonder how difficult the journey to Dadyal must have been. She had by then four young kids: apart from Bhaiji Begum, the eldest child who was six years old, there was my uncle Shafi Ali, four years old, and my father, Munir, and his twin brother, Shabir, just seven months.

My father and his twin nearly died on that trip. The journey itself was difficult. A flight to Lahore then travel by car to Dadyal. My father and Chacha (or uncle) Shabir were in incubators. But in Dadyal they got diarrhoea. Dadyal then was a village with no amenities, not even a doctor. They had to be taken to the nearest city and there the doctors said they were untreatable. They were too weak. They wouldn't survive the journey back to England. The only alternative was to take them to Karachi, Pakistan's largest city, to see a specialist. They got better and eventually made it back to England.

Just over a year later my grandfather decided his children must return to Dadyal to make sure they had a good basic Islamic education. So, my father, aged two, left England and did not return until he was ten. Neither of my grandparents moved to Pakistan. My grandfather continued to work here, going back and forth, staying for months at a time. My father and his siblings were looked after by my great-grandparents. It was what Betty did that showed a great sense of adventure and tremendous courage. While my father was in Dadyal she made five trips there, to a world she had no knowledge of and which to her must have been very strange.

I have often heard the story from my father of seeing his mother arrive in Dadyal for the first time. Buses normally did not come to the village, where most transport was by tonga, a horse-drawn cart. As the bus approached all the kids ran towards it. The sight of the bus made the kids so excited that they tried to jump on board to see this strange machine that had suddenly come into their midst. To them it must have seemed like the scene from Spielberg's *ET* when the kids watch an alien spaceship landing. For my father it was particularly exciting for on the bus was his mother coming all the way from England to see him. He was only five and it had been three years since he had last seen her.

If the bus was alien to the children of the village then for my grandmother life in Dadyal was also very strange. And how she coped with life there was remarkable. In the 1960s Dadyal, which is now a substantial town, had no electricity, running water, paved roads or proper sanitation. For their ablutions people just went outdoors. This Englishwoman from Birmingham, far from being fazed, adjusted to it. One of my dad's cousins was fairly well off and their house was the only one in the village with an inside toilet. They said that as my grandmother was not used to such a rustic life she could come and use the toilet in their house. Sometimes she did but not all the time. She just joined in with the locals. (Ironically, what surprised my dad most about England was to discover that there were houses with outside toilets. He had been brought up to believe that everyone had an ensuite bathroom.)

Dad remembers her going to the river to wash the clothes. There, like the locals, she would bash the clothes against the flat stones along the river bank. I can only marvel how this middle-aged woman, having come from an England where many homes now had a washing machine, instantly took to the traditional launderette of the subcontinent. Nothing in her experience had prepared her for this but she was determined to be part of this world and intelligent enough to know how to do it. For her it was exciting. She enjoyed the experience of learning the ways of this world, so different to her own. Betty told me that when she first arrived there were lots of scorpions in the very basic family house, which terrified her, so a maulana, a Muslim scholar, was called in – once he'd recited his words, she never saw a scorpion again. In an effort to understand the people, she learnt Urdu and while she never spoke it well she could follow conversations. Her willingness to become part of my grandfather's world was greatly appreciated by his family and friends, who all called her Babbhiji and treated her with utmost respect. They recognized that she kept everything together.

Dad did not come back to England until 1966, when he was ten years old. He remembers how frightened he was when the year before there had been war between India and Pakistan over Kashmir and every time the aeroplanes were in the air he and all the kids in the village would run and hide to escape the bombs. He and his siblings spoke Mirpuri, an old language, a cross between Urdu and Punjabi. He knew a bit of Urdu, but only a few words and even that not very well. He could not speak even a single word of English.

When he went to comprehensive school this caused a problem on the very first day. His uncle had told him that he would pick him and Chacha Shabir up at lunchtime and that they should come to the school gate and wait for him. When it came to mid-morning break, not able to follow what was going on and thinking it was lunchtime, the two went to the school gate and waited. They were still there when everybody went back in and when the register was taken in the class they were missing. This started a hunt for them and eventually my father saw a white boy approaching them. Despite the fact that he couldn't follow a word the white boy was saying he understood it was not yet lunchtime and they had to go back to the classroom. It was no easy matter to learn a new language at the age of ten; English for a long time was a foreign tongue for Dad, and it was only by the time that he and his brothers sat their O Levels that they were confident in the language. There was never much money, life was quite hard and Dad would get nervous when speaking: at the age of fifteen he developed a stammer due to stress.

Everything about England was strange and you can hardly blame him for feeling like an outsider. The famous English weather bewildered him. In Dadyal he used to see the sun blaze from a cloudless sky every day, except occasionally during the rainy season. That was hardly worth commenting on. Now he had to get used to the fact that in England if the sun came out it was almost a day of joyous celebration. He had come in April and soon there was summer which did produce sunny days, but when winter came he could not believe how grey and cold it was, even inside the house. That first winter when my father saw snow he had the same feeling that Clive Lloyd had when the great West Indian came to England for the first time to play for Lancashire. Like Lloyd, Dad had never seen snow before and just could not believe these slivers of wispy white paper falling from the sky and covering streets, houses and cars so suddenly that the whole world seemed to have turned white.

Dad did not see much of my grandfather after his return to England from Pakistan. He did not really get to know his father. This was because my grandfather decided to leave Birmingham and go back to Dadyal to look after his parents and settle back in his village, becoming a local politician. He visited occasionally but for much of Dad's youth Pakistan was my grandfather's home. But while Dad only had his mum with him in England it was not the typical single-parent home you might imagine, as the wider family of uncles and aunts all lived together. Often there were visitors who also stayed there for long periods. My grandfather was well known and when people came from Dadyal and they had nowhere to stay they would head for the house in Church Road, Moseley. The doyen of the house was my grand-father's youngest brother, Daulat Ali, who I called Nikka Bhaji, small uncle. By the time I was born he was an old man with kidney trouble but I heard many stories of how he had been a very strict man who laid down the law and had a reputation of never telling a lie. My father, who loved him, says everybody used to come to Nikka Bhaji to ask his advice because they knew he would not waffle but give it straight. Inside the house there was warmth and comfort, a world my grandmother did much to create. It was a big house with seven bedrooms but with so many people living there my father's bedroom was in the attic, which he shared with his two brothers and three other cousins. At weekends many others from Mirpur would come for a meal and my grandmother taught all her children to make tea while she did the cooking. Dad's abiding memory of his mother is in the kitchen at all hours of the day slaving over a hot stove. There were always people to feed and these were lavish meals.

There must have been frustrations though, as my grandpar-ents did separate and Betty moved out when Dad was fourteen, taking Shah Begum with her and leaving her sons behind to be brought up by their uncles, with Daulat Ali their guardian. The extended Asian family system stepped in to make sure my father and his brothers had a nurturing family life. My grandmother moved to another part of Birmingham and away from the Islamic faith, losing touch with her sons for some years, but by the time Dad married they were back in each other's lives and remained in touch till she died. She became a big influence in my life, a very smart, sharp lady who was always smiling. We never celebrated Christmas but, having reverted to Christianity, every year she would send a big bag of Christmas presents which we always looked forward to. I did witness her reuniting with my grandfather, at my house, towards the end of her life. He walked in on his stick and Betty was sitting there on my sofa and said quite cheekily, 'Come here, I'm still your wife' as an ice-breaker. After the tensions following their separation, it was very cathartic for them to meet and forgive each other. They ended up dying within six months of each other. I'm very grateful to have been brought up in a mixed multicultural family – some Asian families are quite insular and feel like all white people are against them which isn't my view at all.

By the time I was born the family had dispersed but we have still remained close and Chacha Shabir is another parent to me, a father-like figure. Every time I see him he reminds me of being a kid – I have a lot of time for people I've known since childhood who make me feel that way. With twin brothers marrying sisters, we all felt like we had two fathers and two mothers. We literally used to all eat off the same plate.

My father has an amazing rapport with his twin. My father was born at ten to one in the afternoon, Chacha Shabir five minutes later. They are so close that they can communicate without writing to each other. If my father is upset Chacha Shabir will instantly know and if he has a problem my father gets very anxious. If one of them grows a moustache, the other one will have to do the same. Even when they are thousands of miles apart there is an extraordinary telepathy between them.

Once when they were fourteen my father had a stomach pain. They took him to hospital and they said it was appendicitis and his appendix had to be removed. When they were operating, Chacha Shabir, thousands of miles away in Pakistan, was in pain. He had a stomach ache and he was crying and shouting. My grandfather was with Chacha and he rang from Pakistan to ask if his twin brother was okay. My great-uncle told him my father had been under the surgeon's knife having his appendix removed. As soon as the surgery was over Chacha Shabir also recovered; later he too had his appendix out.

My father admits that he grew up in a very restrictive household. As he puts it:

We were not allowed to do this, not allowed to do that. We could not talk in front of our elders. We showed respect by being quiet, doing salaams. If our parents and elders said you have got to be back at seven o'clock we had to be back at seven o'clock. Not ten past seven. We used to enjoy watching the cinemas. We were not allowed to go to the cinemas late. We could watch the twelve o'clock or one o'clock show. After four o'clock we were not allowed to go to the cinema. We were not allowed to do a lot of things. We were not allowed to talk to any girls outside the family. That was forbidden. Or go to night clubs. It was school, home and work.

And my grandfather did not encourage my father and his brothers to play cricket, telling them, 'Study. You are wasting your time playing cricket.'

Like that first sight of snow, cricket was also a very new experience. There was no cricket in Dadyal, the main sport there being kabbadi, the great national sport of the subcontinent. Indeed, the first time Dad saw his schoolmates gather on the sports field to play cricket he couldn't work out what they were doing. 'I thought it was the hockey team,' he recalls.

The teacher, Mr Campbell, said we play hockey in winter. In summer, cricket. Then I saw these kids putting pads on. I asked what are they doing? Then I saw someone run in to bowl. I had never seen a cricket ball before. I was shown how to put the pads on and initially I was a mainly medium pace bowler who could bat. I learnt I could swing the ball and at the beginning when I batted I just swung the bat. But towards the end of my days at school at the age of sixteen I was the main batter for the school team. As I got better and better I got more interested and began to hero worship some players. I wasn't aware of any English players at that time. The players I looked up to were Majid Khan who was playing for Glamorgan, Sunil Gavaskar and Sarfraz Nawaz who was with Northamptonshire. What helped me was that cricket was on the BBC. BBC1 showed every Test match and on Sundays BBC2 had the forty-over John Player League.

That the BBC helped my dad develop his love for cricket shows how things have changed since the 1960s – and not for the better. Then a ten-year-old who did not know cricket existed could get hooked on it because he could watch every ball of the highest form of this greatest of all games. I am full of admiration for what Sky has done, how it has revolutionized cricket coverage and the vast amount of money they have poured into the game. But the fact is that with no live cricket on terrestrial television a ten-year-old just cannot get that vital exposure to cricket that my dad had. Surveys show fewer schools play cricket now and the game is less popular among the young than it was when my father took to cricket back in 1966. Fewer of them play the game. It is interesting that for all its satellite exposure, football still has *Match of the Day* on BBC1. This is why I welcome the return of live cricket to the BBC from 2020. And had my dad not fallen in love with the game on the BBC he would never have worked so hard to make me a cricketer.

CHAPTER 2

THE BOY FROM SPARKHILL

have to thank the Birmingham police for my birth and although I have heard the story often every time I hear it again it feels like a scene from a Bollywood movie.

It is a summer's night in June 1987, around ten o'clock. Chacha Shabir has come to our house in Durham Road with his family. He lives a mile away and asks my dad to drop him home. But Dad is tired, the night is warm, and he doesn't want to go anywhere. He says to Chacha Shabir, 'Take the car.' My mother, Maqsood, is heavily pregnant and Chacha says, 'You might need the car with Maqsood.' Dad says, 'Don't worry, it won't happen today.' Chacha drives off. At 2 a.m. my mother's waters break. Dad immediately rings Chacha Shabir. He's at his wits' end, at a loss as to what to do. Eventually he literally jumps out of the house and runs all the way to Chacha Shabir's house to pick up the keys, drives home, gets Mum to lie down on the back seat and takes her to hospital. He drives like fury and his only thought is of getting to the hospital before she gives birth. But he has to stop for petrol. As he accelerates away from the petrol station a police car stops him. 'Help me,' he pleads, 'my wife is in labour in the back seat.' The police officer looks at my dad disbelievingly. He has heard many excuses for speeding but this is a new one. Dad looks at him imploringly, points to the back seat and one look at Mum's prostrate figure is enough to convince the policeman that Dad is not lying. He nods. 'Follow me', he says, puts the siren on and drives off with my dad following him, no longer worried how fast he drives. The convoy head to the Queen Elizabeth Hospital. As soon as it arrives in the driveway of the hospital the policeman jumps out of the car and runs in. Within minutes a couple of nurses come out with a trolley – Dad thinks the policeman must have alerted the hospital by radio on the way there. As they wheel Mum into the hospital she gives birth to me on the trolley.

My dad always wanted a son called Omar but just before I was born he was playing cricket with a friend called Moeen Mumtaz who suggested he name his son after him. It seemed appropriate as the very day I was born I was introduced to the game of cricket. My dad had long worked on these plans and the moment he knew that he had a son he put them in motion. He had got the idea from Chacha Shabir. The Muslim tradition is that when a boy or a girl is born, a relative, usually an uncle or some other elder of the family, says 'azan', an Arabic word meaning 'listen', to confirm they are Muslim. They put a paper to the ears of the child and say, 'Allah O Akbar, Allah O Akbar, Allah O Akbar, Allah O Akbar.' 'God is greatest.' Seven years before, an uncle in the family did just that when my cousin Kabir was born. As soon as he had finished chanting, Chacha Shabir took out a cricket ball he had in his pocket and rubbed it on

Kabir's forehead. The uncle was very surprised and said, 'What are you doing?' Chacha Shabir said, 'I am writing his *takkdir*, his fate, so that he becomes a fast bowler.' The uncle just looked at him and shook his head in bewilderment. Chacha Shabir had planned this very carefully and had told Dad before the birth of Kabir, 'If I have a boy I will make him a fast bowler.' Chacha Shabir was successful, for Kabir became a fast bowler and played for England. He did the same for his other son Aatif who also became a bowler.

But while, as we have seen, Dad and Chacha Shabir have this incredible empathy, and always know what the other is thinking or feeling, in this instance they disagreed. Dad had decided he wanted his sons to be batsmen. So when Kadeer, who is five years older than me, was born Dad took a little kids' bat to the hospital on the day of his birth and rubbed it on his forehead. Now he did the same with me. And he was to do the same when my little brother Omar as born. And we all became batsmen. Not that I did not like bowling. Indeed, I started as a bowler and a fast bowler at that. How quite by chance I became an off-spinner is a story I shall talk about later.

I was always a great extrovert, very outgoing. But at times it seemed this exuberant spirit went over the top. Dad says of the three of us, Kadeer, Omar and me, I was the one who was 'really naughty'. I was always fighting with Kadeer and Omar, and running around the house doing silly things. I used to wrestle a lot with Omar. I was always the Rock and he was Stone Cold Steve Austin. I hated losing, which is why I was the

Rock while Omar, who always lost, was Stone Cold. Dad would often get exasperated and shout, 'Moeen, what are you doing?' I was then about three or four years old and loved wearing a jacket while I was being 'naughty'. My family nicknamed me Bazooka. The name came from a Bollywood movie where one of the tough guys, played by the Hindi film star Dharmendra, was called Bazooka. My family still talk about Bazooka when they talk of my younger days.

If I was an unruly child, at my secondary school I became even more of a rebel. Perhaps that's a bit harsh on myself. Not so much a rebel wanting to tear things down, but let's say I had the guts to break a few more rules than many of my friends. I was suspended three times.

I did calm down and football helped with that, at least as far as my dad and the family were concerned. Although it was a cricket bat not a football that was rubbed on my forehead on the day of my birth, from a very early age I took to the national game. Kadeer was a Liverpool supporter and I followed my big brother's example and made the Reds my team. Kids follow success. Liverpool then were in their prime and, like my role model Robbie Fowler, I loved playing as a forward and scoring goals. Had Mohamed Salah been playing for Liverpool then I would have made him my role model and tried to bulge the net in the way he did so magnificently during the 2017–18 season. Now I was the Bazooka on the football field instead of at home. Omar, who was born a year later, grew up just as Manchester United under Sir Alex Ferguson had begun their remarkable rise and overshadowed Liverpool, so he decided to follow the Reds of Manchester. Now, Dad is not much interested in football and if he has a team it is Birmingham City. But because Kadeer and I loved Liverpool, along with my mum and sister Asba, Dad decided to become a United supporter to give Omar a little more support.

If football quietened me round the house it did not mean I lost my competitive edge. I learnt how to channel that desire to be competitive. But however passionate I was and remain in my support for Liverpool, I never saw myself as a professional footballer. In a reversal of what the Neville brothers, Gary and Phil, did, both of whom were good cricketers, I made cricket not football my main game and the centre of my life. And I took to it in a very Birmingham version of the way cricketers in the subcontinent learn the game.

In the cities and towns of the subcontinent kids hone their skills by playing what are called building matches, where the building they live in plays against another building. In the Sparkhill area of south Birmingham, and particularly in Stoney Lane where I grew up, there are no high-rise buildings as can be found in Mumbai but row after row of run-down terraced houses. My introduction to competitive cricket was through lane cricket. I lived on Stoney Lane and we had a Stoney Lane team. A neighbouring street was Brunswick Road and we played them often. But the derby game was against Fulham Road. Stoney Lane joins Fulham Road and for us Fulham Road was always the showpiece match of our lane competition when no quarter was asked and none given.

As time went on we used to play parks in the area. Further down was Broseley Park. They used to come over and we used to go there, home and away fixtures. This may not be how many people take to cricket – inner-city cricket is still not that common – but as crazy as it sounds the matches were amazing. There were no trophies, just bragging rights and the intense competitiveness we showed during the matches. I have never had more fun playing cricket.

My passion for cricket developed despite the fact that my primary school, where I started going to nursery at the age of three, in 1990, did not play cricket. Now a declining number of schools play cricket, often because they have sold off their playing fields. My school had no facilities to play cricket. Nevertheless, I should make it clear that I have very fond memories of Nelson Mandela Community Primary School, named in memory of a man who has been described as the only political saint of our times. His visit to our school in 1993 was memorable. I had the honour to meet him many years later when I went to South Africa. Today, if you go the school you see his picture by the entrance and below it a sign with Mandela saying, 'We know too well that our freedom is incomplete without the freedom of the Palestinians.' Those are noble sentiments and ones I share.

The school also taught me how cosmopolitan the world we live in is. We had such a salad bowl of people from different religions and colours. We had Arabs, people of Pakistani backgrounds, from all sorts of other cultures and backgrounds and also white people. We all got on and it taught me that nobody should care what colour a person is or what religion. Everybody is a human being. I was raised to mix and feel normal and be a straight sort of person. I feel safer living in a community like this than going to a posher area. Growing up like this has taught me to be open-minded about people's origins.

However, there was nowhere in the school we could play cricket. When my father took Kadeer to the school a teacher said, 'We don't play cricket. We only play soccer.' But – and this is what makes Stoney Lane so special for me – there was still a place we could play and what is more it helped me develop into the batsman I have become. In the subcontinent youngsters play what they call 'gully' cricket. A gully is a little alleyway off the main street, often a dead end where the players mark the wickets on the wall with a chalk and play cricket. So no cricket at school, but in Stoney Lane, a one-minute walk from where we lived, we made our own version of gully cricket Sparkhill-style.

It was an enclosed place decorated with an arch. A sign in Urdu and Bengali said, 'Please do not feed the pigeons'. This was good for it meant the pigeons didn't disrupt the games we played. The space, about the size of an Olympic swimming pool, provided us a rough tarmac surface bounded by walls of different heights, coloured in various hues and full of graffiti. For a wicket we used to borrow a milk crate from a grocery shop down Stoney Lane and put it up against one of the walls. It was a bit wider than a normal set of stumps but at least it meant that when someone got in you had a chance of getting him out. Obviously, there were no bails, nor could there be a wicket keeper behind the stumps, but the rule was if you nicked it on to the wall you were out. Even when we played a Test match, of two innings a side, a good total was 120 or 130. The square-leg umpire sat on one of the walls and, as you would expect in such games, the umpires were from the team batting so there was, I confess, a bit of cheating sometimes.

Sachin Tendulkar has said that he learnt to keep the ball on the ground because if he hit the ball in the air it could break one of the windows of the building he lived in. In my case the enclosed space taught me how to cover-drive well. One of the walls had a gap where cover would be on a traditional cricket ground and I enjoyed hitting the ball through that opening. And the setting of this enclosed space bound by roads also improved my leg-side play. When I was twelve or thirteen I could not play off my hips. I ended up practising with Kadeer, Omar, Kabir and Aatif. I imagined I was playing in a Test match. Brunswick Road was the leg-side boundary. I saw Brunswick Road as a target to aim for and soon I was hitting the ball so hard it always bounced on the tarmac every time the ball connected with the meat of my bat. From a player who could not hit the ball on the leg-side I became the classical left-hander who could always milk runs if a ball was pitched on his legs. It's strange: I can't do anything else with my left hand apart from batting. When you're batting your top hand is supposed to be the strongest, so I feel I bat the right way round.

It was only years later when I started playing county cricket that I realized how much I had learnt as a kid playing in that enclosed place at Stoney Lane. I suppose it showed I was streetwise and could use whatever resources were available to improve myself.

Kadeer first played with a hard ball for the Warwickshire Under-11s. I did not play hard-ball cricket until I was nine years old. I was introduced to the game very much in the Pakistani style with a rubber ball taped up. As we were playing without pads a hard ball would have been very dangerous and would certainly have put me off cricket.

My cricketing heroes were the men who dominated the game when I was growing up: Viv Richards, Ian Botham, Saeed Anwar and above all Brian Lara. I just loved the way Lara would take the bowling apart. Ricky Ponting, comparing Lara with Tendulkar, has said that when he was captain, if he knew Lara was batting the next day he would have a sleepless night worrying how he would get him out. But while he would respect what Tendulkar might do, he would always sleep well the night before he was to bat. Lara could turn a game and win it for his side in the way nobody else has. I always saw myself as an opener; when I was batting, I was Marcus Trescothick. I think he was the first England opener that I can remember coming out and really taking the bowling on. I watched him and thought, Wow!

I also bowled although the setting of our cricket meant you could not bowl spin. You couldn't bowl spin because you would be smacked everywhere. Pace would deter the batsmen in a way spin could not. I cannot think of anyone in our Lane teams that bowled spin. In the Lane matches all of us boys would run in and bowl fast. I did the same. I used to run in and bowl as fast as I could.

Cricket's greatest impact on me was that it saved me from a life of drugs and crime. The surrounding area round Stoney Lane was rough, with classic inner-city problems we read so much about. This was a neighbourhood that was violent. Just down from where we played cricket was a roundabout, a place called Churchyard. I remember there used to be fights almost every day down there, lots of crime and you'd always hear stories of awful things happening. As a kid I saw loads of fights. Beyond our Olympic-sized cricket pitch there was a field and a few gangs would congregate there; they were very tough guys – they played cricket as well. It wasn't like it is now where people have knives – it was a proper fight, a pitch fight. But these guys did carry all sorts of weapons. They had with them objects which they could spin around and horrible weapons like metal bars. I used to find it quite frightening when I was young, seeing grown men fighting. I remember once they just charged a couple of guys who were playing cricket. Me and my brother just ran. It was scary. But after a while I got used to it. Obviously I didn't like seeing such fights but it became quite a normal thing. I was very fortunate because my friends, as soon they saw fighting break out, used to say, 'Look, you play cricket, we don't want you to join in. We don't want you to take part in it.' However, because they were my best friends I felt I should do something or help them. Initially I always tried to stop the fights, not often successfully, but I managed not to get involved in them. I was determined to be a cricketer and that vision of playing professionally kept me going and kept me grounded. Some of my friends, sad to say, did not have that outlet. They didn't know what they wanted to be. They got caught and as soon as you get caught it is very difficult to come out of it. And some of my friends took recreational drugs. There were times when I thought I'd love to try them too. I was tempted, yes, of course I was.

I was dragged away from temptation by the lure of getting back to our own gully cricket, the special cricket ground and playing the game. Where we played cricket there were no fights; if there was violence, it was sorted out. Once a guy hit another guy and I saw one of the senior guys go up to him. He never raised his hands, hit him or anything. He just warned the guy and it didn't happen again. It was that sort of place. This was our go-to place. It was also where we went if we had problems at school. And I had trouble at school. Every time I was suspended, my response was always to play more cricket. I couldn't wait to go outside to play. Dinner time, anytime we could, I would rush out to play. I would spend all day playing till the sun set and then go home. Sometimes my mum would take us to the mosque. After that we would do a U-turn and head straight back to play cricket. We would play not only all summer long but also in the winter and only stop if football was buzzing. Or, of course, when Liverpool were on the telly.

We used to have lights, and in the holidays we'd come straight away in the morning, just go home for a quick lunch and come back out, and wouldn't finish till the evening. I absolutely loved it.

I have played in the best, greatest grounds of the world, grounds which were just names to me when I was growing up. But the Stoney Lane ground compares with Lord's, Oval, Melbourne, Sydney, Mumbai, Barbados, or any other historic ground you care to name. I have always felt if I ever became a county player or played for England I would never change or feel bigger than anybody else. I come back to Stoney Lane every year. There is a ten-over-a-team competition here. Kids from all over the county come. A couple of thousand people gather. Since I started playing for England my presence here creates pressure from people wanting to meet me because I am an England player. I must confess I do feel the pressure. It would be easy to keep away. But I continue to come because I am still part of the community. As I see it I was coming back to this community even after I started playing county cricket and before I played for England. I don't see why I should stop now. When I come back to this place where it all started it does not feel real that I am an England player. That I'm here one day and next day playing in front of thousands at the Oval or Lord's. Playing for England regularly for the last three or four years makes me feel so fortunate. I still can't believe I am playing for England.

That Stoney Lane upbringing where cricket was so central

has left me with great memories. Even now when I drive past I wish those days would come back. That time in my life, those days were so special. I know I shall never again experience that wonderful bliss. No worries about anything. You just played cricket. You went home. You looked forward to the next day because you would do exactly the same thing. My memories of those days are so strong that whenever I think about them I get a warm feeling inside me. Sometimes you get caught in things and forget where you are from. You forget your friends. I have tried never to do that. It helps that some of the same guys I grew up and played cricket with still live on Stoney Lane. It is years since I moved away from Stoney Lane. I live in a very different environment now – though not far away – but in my mind I have never left this area. I shall always belong to Stoney Lane. I shall always be the boy from Sparkhill. I may have moved away from Sparkhill but nothing can take Sparkhill from me.

I was eleven when I left Nelson Mandela to go to Moseley school. The change was dramatic. For a start as you approached Moseley you saw a fine, imposing Victorian building, with archways and several modern buildings linked to this main one. There was a cricket ground. Today visitors to the ground may feel it looks rough and the wicket appears to be a bit dodgy but for me it was heaven. This was my first proper ground with its own pavilion. It helped that we had a sports teacher, Mr Manda, who encouraged us to play cricket and made me feel I was exceptional. This is when for the first time I thought I might become a professional cricketer. It was all cricket for me now. I just wasn't interested in my studies and after about a year at Moseley, when I was twelve, I told Dad, 'Dad don't expect me to get my GCSEs. I am not going to get them. I want to be a professional sportsman.'

I must confess I did not care for books and the classroom. I had to do my GCSE exams in 1995. I told my teacher, 'I don't want to do it. I can't do it.'. The teacher forced me to take the exams. I must confess when it comes to books I have never been the brightest.

Had my father been like many other Asian fathers he would have reacted angrily, perhaps even slapped me. But Dad's reaction was very different. He was overjoyed and excited. Those were just the words he wanted to hear. He knew what was required to make me a cricketer and was prepared to make sure I became one. Without him it wouldn't have happened.

CHAPTER 3

CHICKENS AND CRICKET

t would have been so easy for my dad to be a conventional Asian father. My parents had married in what was the classical subcontinental arrangement. In 1979 Dad, then aged twenty-four, went back to Pakistan along with Chacha Shabir. His grandmother had selected brides for both of them. It could not be neater. There were two sisters from a family in the village she knew well. The entire village and many people from surrounding areas and even some from cities which were quite a distance away came to the wedding. Dad rode a horse to my mum's place and it was only on the wedding night that he first set eyes on her. Three months later he returned to Birmingham and my mum followed in April 1980 with her sister now married to Chacha Shabir.

By then Dad was a nurse. In reality what he wanted was to be a professional cricketer. But he had no encouragement from his family. He was constantly told by my grandfather and his uncles that there was no point playing cricket and he grew up hearing the refrain so many children hear from their mums and dads in Asian households: 'my son the engineer, my son the doctor', pushing them hard to get a qualification in these professions. Dad faced this pressure constantly and had to give in. He did not want to be a doctor but liked the medical field. At school he was interested in human biology and decided he would become a nurse. Immediately on leaving school he actually worked in a hospital, as a porter at Moseley Hall Hospital, a specialist neurological rehabilitation unit. He eventually, after a great deal of struggle and no little effort, qualified as a nurse. He was always aware that his background and skin colour made him different and when he went to work he always wore a three-piece suit and took very good care of how he looked.

It was some years after my birth, when Dad was in his forties, that he realized what a talented cricketer he was, how he could have been wearing whites rather than a nurse's uniform and how different things could have been had he had coaching and been given the opportunities to play the game when he was young. Such was his love for cricket that as we were growing up Dad was always going off at weekends to various parts of the country wherever he could get a game. He was a member of a team of local Pakistani boys called CBP, City of Birmingham Pakistanis. Many of the members of the team were factory workers. CBP played in the Birmingham Parks League. Dad opened the batting and was the key player in his side, the player the team relied on. He showed a natural aptitude for playing fast bowling. This was not run-of-the-mill league cricket but high-standard cricket where he often faced international players, some of whom had played Test cricket for various countries. Dad regularly scored runs against them. In one match in Huddersfield he faced Raja Azeem Hafeez, a fast bowler who, despite the fact that he had two fingers missing from his right hand, played 18 Tests for Pakistan and might have played more but for the fact that this was the era of Wasim Akram. The team Dad faced also had seven or eight other Pakistanis who had played first-class cricket. In this match Dad opened the batting for his side and made 92, scoring heavily off Hafeez's bowling. Dad recalls how it was a beautiful summer's day, good for batting and afterwards, when he was told that Hafeez was about to go to Pakistan for trials, he burst out laughing, unable to believe that a bowler he had despatched to every corner of the ground could be a Test cricketer.

Perhaps the match that summed up Dad's ability was early in his playing days when he faced the young Colin Croft, part of that remarkable West Indian armoury of fast bowlers that spearheaded Clive Lloyd's side, the greatest in the history of the game. Croft, yet to make his Test debut and on a scholarship at Warwickshire, opened the bowling and Dad, once again opening the batting for his team, pulled him, getting a top edge for six. Also playing in the match was another West Indian fast bowler called Jackson who while not quite as pacy as Croft, was also sharp. Dad wasn't wearing a helmet but this didn't worry him. In another match, the final of a 20-over tournament, Dad top-edged a ball into his eye, had to go to hospital, and required six stitches. But he came back and faced the bowling despite having to bat with one eye shut. Injuries never bothered him. It was after one of these matches that he told me,

'Oh, if I was young now and had a bit of coaching I would be playing international cricket.'

When my dad tells his cricket stories he really puffs up his chest, and is always keen to tell us how good he was. My older brother Kadeer will ask him, 'Were you better than me?' and he'll say no. I'll ask him the same thing and get the same answer. But then my younger brother, Omar, will say, 'Dad, were you better than me' and my dad always gets a gleam in his eye like he thinks he could take him … then Omar rolls his eyes and says 'Dad, I don't think so.' Once my sister Azba was at one of his games and not paying attention – my dad shouted her name and then hit the ball so it landed right in her face. I think he found it funnier than she did.

Dad was determined that Kadeer and I would not miss out on the coaching and the encouragement that he lacked. This meant standing up to the wider family of uncles and his own father who could see no merit in sport. They kept telling Dad that it was a waste of time encouraging us to play cricket. They kept repeating, 'There is no career in it.' Dad's response was, 'Oh, they are going to do something special.' Dad was convinced we could make it as professional players if we got the chance to prove ourselves. What he wanted to do was help open doors for us. By the time I was seven Kadeer was already playing in his age group for Warwickshire and it was only natural that I wanted to follow in his footsteps.

The first door Dad opened for me was when I was nine. The trials were on for the Warwickshire Under-11 team at Edgbaston.

Dad drove me there and when we got to the indoor school he spoke to David Parsons, who is now the Performance Director with the England team. Dad, who knew him a bit, said, 'I have brought Moeen,' as if he was giving Parsons a present. Parsons shook his head, 'This is the final day of the trials. The team is about to be selected. It's too late.' Then looking at me he said, 'He is a bit too young and small at the moment.' Dad, who is the most dogged, persistent person I have ever met, never takes no for an answer and replied, 'I have brought his kit. I want you have a look at him.' Parsons realized he could not fob Dad off and said in a rather resigned voice, 'Okay. Let's have look at him.' I was asked to bowl. Dad, who could bowl quick and often opened the bowling for his team, had coached me to make sure I had a classical fast bowler's action. Dad had also shown me how to move the ball. I did not have a fast bowler as my role model although I liked the way Glenn McGrath played.

I knew Parsons was looking at me and I was determined to make an impression. I ran in and after a mighty jump delivered the ball as fast as I could. From the expression on Dad's face I knew that I had bowled well. Parsons must have thought so as well, although at this stage he said nothing. With only five minutes of the net session remaining I was asked to pad up. They were not my pads but belonged to Taheer Nakash, the son of a friend of Dad's. He was a right-hander, I was of course left-handed and as I was so small they came up almost to my stomach. As I padded up I made up my mind about how I was going to bat. Many of the boys in the nets were much bigger than me, some of them had been playing for the county already, but I decided I was not going to defend. I was going to bat as if this was no different to our ground in Stoney Lane. I was going to hit the ball and show them I could clobber any bowling. That is exactly what I did. I could see that Parsons was watching me very carefully and as the session finished he came up to Dad and said, 'Munir, you knew he was good.' My dad, glowing with pride, said, 'I know he is good.' But Parsons explained that he had a problem. 'He is very young,' he said. 'We have almost selected the side. What we will do is pick him for the reserves. We'll keep him in the team and next year he will be okay.' That proved very helpful. I went to all the training games and even played four matches that year.

The big moment was when I played against the Lancashire Under-11s. The match was in Manchester and we travelled by coach. I had never left Birmingham, never been in a coach before. Some of the kids had their parents travelling with them. But Dad couldn't go because Kadeer was also playing and he had to take him to his match. He saw me off as I left my family for the first time. On the way there I kept looking out of the window at the lush countryside, this beautiful, green and pleasant land of ours which for someone brought up in Sparkhill was like another world. However, my thoughts were on cricket and what I would do when I got to bat. By the time I arrived at the ground near Old Trafford I was clear in my mind. I would treat this match like a derby against Fulham Road. I would hit the ball as far and as hard as I could. I shall never forget the moment when I hit one of the Lancashire bowlers for a huge six. I could not wait to tell Dad. And all the way back I thought of the moment I would tell him. It was nearly eight o'clock in the evening when the bus pulled into the Edgbaston ground, just outside the outdoor school. I could see Dad waiting with the other parents. I jumped out of the bus and with my arms raised ran to Dad shouting, 'Dad, I hit a six!' Everybody started laughing. But they were not mocking me. They were sharing my joy. I could see the pride in his face. All our hours of hard work were paying off.

Next year I started playing in my age group but I was soon moved up from the Under-11s to Under-12s. For Dad this meant tremendous additional work. He was now taking both Kadeer and me to Edgbaston three or four times a week. Dad even took me to Worcestershire for coaching with the great Basil D'Oliveira. It cost a lot of money. I am aware this is what parents keen to develop their kids' talent do. But Dad decided that it was not enough to be a conventional parent and just ferry me and Kadeer to Edgbaston for coaching. Let him take up the story:

I wanted to do something that nobody else does. We had to have coaching at home. I spoke to Shabir and decided we would get a bowling machine. Money was hard to come by. We borrowed some money and bought a machine. Shabir had bought a large house in Fulham Road. It had a big garden. We dug up the garden and put up the nets there and bought a mat. It cost us £3,000. This meant we had our own training facility. So they could go to school, come back and instead of going to Edgbaston they could have a net in the garden. We also used the bowling machine inside the house. We put it in a room in the house but turned the speed knob to slow. Sometimes we used to do underarm throws to the boys. We worked extremely hard until it got dark and we were not able to see the ball. We were using the bowling machine all the time. It was cricket for breakfast, cricket for lunch and cricket for tea. And we used to sit at the dining table at home and discuss all the matches and everything related to cricket. Moeen and the boys used to go and play football sometimes, they had their own team, but it was cricket, cricket, cricket. I wanted my children to play for England and was determined to do everything to make that possible.

The bowling machine also travelled with us in our car as we drove around the Midlands from one town to another playing cricket. I remember once we were going to Tipton which is a fair drive from where we were in Birmingham. Six of us were packed in that old Toyota. Chacha Shabir was driving, Dad was in the front passenger seat, Kadeer, Kabir, Omar and myself were squashed in at the back. It was a tight squeeze. In addition to the cricket bags there was also the bowling machine and the balls you feed into the machine. But that day we couldn't find the indoor school at Tipton. As we hunted for the place

Chacha Shabir couldn't change the gear. The car stalled so he pressed the clutch and Dad started changing gear. Eventually we found the indoor facility, set up the bowling machine and had a training session. The drive had taken us an hour and half and we didn't return home until midnight. But that sort of thing happened often and I recall with great affection many such journeys in the Toyota carrying the bowling machine with us and trying to find a place to practise.

Dad wanted to spend all his time with me and Kadeer as he was convinced both of us would play for England. Let him tell you how he felt about the two of us:

I wanted one of my boys to play for England. Kadeer was naturally very, very talented. He was so elegant, I thought he would open the batting in a Test match for England. It was beautiful to watch him play. Even now it is. I found Moeen different. He had that Asian style of playing. Fluent. No worries. No fear. But he also had a bit of English in him. Kadeer was more typical English. Playing straight, playing in the V. Moeen used to go wherever the ball was. He would pick the ball from outside the off-stump and heave it to the leg side. He reminded me of Vivian Richards. My all-time favourite. I was confident Moeen would make it.

However, as we started to play for the Warwickshire youth teams Dad had a problem. By this time he had a very good nursing job. He was in his forties and had reached that stage in his career where, if he stayed and carried on, he could consolidate his career prospects and make sure he retired from the profession in comfort. Now keen to promote our cricket prospects he would drive me or Kadeer to various matches and was constantly juggling his duties as a nurse to make sure we did not miss cricket. Once he was on night duty. The next day I was playing for the Warwickshire Under-13s in Nottingham. So he came home and, without having had any sleep, drove me to Nottingham which took a good hour and a half. We returned late in the evening. He just had time to eat some food that my mum had prepared before he was back in the car driving to work. A day later he was taking Kadeer to a match. Once he spent the entire week with me or Kadeer taking us to matches at Edgbaston or Nottingham and wherever else we played. He was tiring himself out and beginning to feel ill. He suffered headaches and wasn't feeling very well at all. But there was no let-up.

One day he was taking Kadeer to Handsworth Grammar School and felt a bit uneasy while driving, sweaty, feeling not right, feeling funny in his body. He stopped the car for ten or fifteen minutes, then drove on again and got to Handsworth. It was a long drive made worse by the morning rush-hour traffic. Having dropped Kadeer he drove back although he stopped on the way. When he got home he told Mum, 'I don't know what happened.' He went to his doctor to check his blood pressure and it was so sky high they called an ambulance. He went to Hartland Hospital and they said that Dad was very lucky. They thought he was going to have a stroke. His face was going a bit funny. He could feel something going on his head, pins and needles in his face. They shifted him to a ward, put him to bed and wouldn't let him get out of the bed at all. Not even to go to the toilet. He was not even allowed to stand up or do anything as his blood pressure was so high. It was six or seven days by the time they let him get up from the bed. He was in the hospital for about a week or ten days. I went to visit him and we were all very worried about him.

It was clear he could not be a full-time nurse and help us reach that cricketing peak he wanted us to. Either it was his job or me and Kadeer playing cricket. I can think of many fathers who at this stage would have decided they could not afford to take their sons to cricket. I wouldn't blame them. But my dad was different. He had set his heart on either Kadeer or me playing for England. So, after much agonizing in 2000, when I was thirteen years old, he gave up nursing and decided that his career from now on would be to make sure that one of us played for England. It was a momentous decision. History is littered with parents making great sacrifices for their children but I cannot think of a greater one than the one my dad made. Not that he had money in the bank. It was financially hard and initially he started doing bits and bobs of work, fitting them to our cricket schedule. But this proved a nightmare and he decided the only way to make ends meet would be to sell chickens.

Imagine. The new millennium has just dawned. Dad and Chacha Shabir drive to an abattoir and buy whole chickens, fifty, sixty of them, once a hundred chickens, put them in the boot of the old Toyota and drive home. There in the shed, which has been kept clean, they cut the chickens up, put them in bags and sell them door to door. Dad made £1 each on every chicken he sold. He could never sell more than hundred on any given day so the most he could make was £100. Back in the days when my grandfather came here from the subcontinent Muslims in this country had done that. Then there were very few Muslims, no Halal butchers and they would buy chickens and slaughter them in the Halal way. But that was to observe religious laws. Now Dad was doing it to make enough money so me and Kadeer could one day play cricket for England.

By this time our family circumstances had changed. As a child I had grown up in a large house in Durham Road. But although it had five bedrooms it was crowded as all the uncles lived there. I shared a bedroom with Kadeer, Omar and three cousins. But then as the uncles moved away we moved to a smaller house in Stoney Lane. With Kadeer now playing county cricket he got one of the bedrooms. My sister Azba, who I call Azba Bajii, had her own bedroom and I shared the smaller bedroom with Omar. But the real sacrifice was made by Mum and Dad. They slept in the downstairs reception room. But such hardship did not mean we were in any way unhappy. We understood why this was being done. It was for our good and we never made demands that our parents could not meet. All of us understood the bigger picture.

What sustained me was that Dad was always encouraging me. He would say, 'Moeen, there is nobody like you. You are completely different. You have the elegance, talent and every-thing. Work hard, work hard. Moeen, you set your goals. The goal must be defeat the champions. If you are going to beat somebody, if you are going to compare yourself with anybody, it's got to be the champion, it's no use doing it with the second class, you've got to get to the top.' Dad had done a lot of reading of books on psychology and told me, 'Moeen, obsta-cles are what you create when you take your eyes off your own goals but if you set your own goals all your obstacles will go away.' Dad always knew that to get the best from somebody you do not reprimand, or wield the rod, but make them believe they are best.

It was soon after moving to Stoney Lane that he sat me down and had a conversation with me which for me was a game changer, the turning point in my cricketing career. It ensured that I would become a professional cricketer.

'You give me two years of your life and I will give you the rest of your life,' he said.

I was surprised. 'What do you mean, Dad?'

'For two years do what I want you to do,' he replied. 'I will sacrifice my two years for you. We work hard together. If nothing works after two years the rest of it is your life. Do whatever you want. We need to do something now. If you're going to play cricket, it's all cricket. I will guide you, I'll work with you, I'll give you everything right, but two years, no friends, you're not going out with friends, you've got to stop all that because it's twenty-four-hour cricket. You play cricket at school, you play for the club, you play county cricket, we'll practise at home. Breakfast, lunch, evening; it's all about cricket and focusing on how to go forward.'

So keen was Dad to learn that he did a diploma in sports psychology, learning how to win. One of the books he was reading then was called *Mind Over Matter*. He emphasized to me that in the past sportspeople didn't look at psychology, but all sport is about psychology, and cricket more than most. He had also started level two coaching courses at Edgbaston.

He felt that while people playing cricket were taught how to bowl and bat, what they didn't know was the psychological side. How to overcome the stress and the mental barriers. What he did now was to talk to me all about the positives. There was no such thing as a failure or going left or right, it was all about going straight.

He emphasized to me that I had the skill to compete but what I must aim to do is become a champion. 'Work so hard that you defeat the champions. To beat the champion you need to be mentally very strong. Okay, you have the skill, but if you have the skill and you get nervous or if you have the skill and you let other obstacles come in your way, then that skill won't work. But if you can add the psychological side, the body needs to be calm, your mind calm, you'll be able to compete with the best and beat the champions. If you just play in the final, people won't talk about the finalists; they all talk about the winner, and that's what you want to be, the winner.'

What had convinced Dad of my skill was an innings I had played when I had just turned thirteen in 2000. It came during a match I played for the Moseley Ashfield Cricket Club. It is not like the much bigger club with the same name in Solihull that was a founding member of the Birmingham League, or Walmley Cricket Club in Sutton Coldfield, which claims to be the biggest cricket club in the Midlands. Before I went to Moseley Ashfield my Dad took me to play at West Brom Dartmouth. For some reason the kids were asked to pick the teams and I didn't know anyone so I was one of the last kids chosen which was frustrating as I knew I was one of the better players. I'll never forget that awful feeling of standing there waiting to be picked, so I was much happier to be playing for Moseley Ashfield.

Moseley Ashfield is small but in an utterly charming setting with the ground surrounded by trees, something you would not expect in inner-city Birmingham. It was the first time I played cricket on a nicely maintained lush green field, with a big white sight screen and outside the clubhouse a bench where Omar and I often sat when we were playing. The clubhouse has a photo of Dad sitting next to me on the bench, wearing dark glasses and looking very pensive. The wicket was good for batting, a batsman could enjoy it particularly if he was prepared to hit the ball. I loved the club and in particular Trevor, who was in charge of the youth team and took me under his wing. A lovely guy. If my dad could not take us, Trevor, who lived nearby, would pick us up. He would always encourage me. People in such positions as Trevor can sometimes try to change young players' style, curb their natural aggressive instincts but Trevor thought it was wonderful that

I was always ready to hit the ball. I often see him now and he tells me how impressed he was when he saw me, just turned eleven: if I faced a bad ball, he says, even if it was the first ball I faced, I wanted to hit it for six, even though I wasn't very big. 'There was not much of you. But you hit the ball so effortlessly. The way you went out to bat and made big runs and made them quickly was wonderful.' When I got out he felt I could have batted all afternoon. He thought I had it in me to become an international player but my mindset then was all about just playing my best and enjoying my cricket.

The innings that I am talking about had been preceded by my first experience of mind games. At that stage I had read about how football managers indulged in mind games before a match to try and unsettle the opposition. Sir Alex Ferguson was the great master of it. It used to upset me when he did it before Manchester United played Liverpool, although in a few years José Mourinho would probably outdo him. But to read about it is one thing; to experience it first hand is something very different. We were playing the Blossomfield Under-15 side, a cricket club based in Solihull. It was a home match. The night before the match Blossomfield's opening bowler Zeeshan, the son of Dad's friend, came to our house, with his father, Asad Ali. He was also of Pakistani origin and they had a very friendly chat over the tea and snacks my mum provided, the conversation alternating between English and Mirpuri. The father had not seen me play. Zeeshan, a left-arm seamer, had in the previous match got a few of the county players out and Asad Ali told Dad he was confident he would take my wicket. They laughed and joked. He was encouraging his son by telling him where to bowl at me. Dad thought Zeeshan would have a few tricks up his sleeve. After they had gone Dad told me, 'Don't get out to him. Be careful with him for the first over or so.'

The match was in the evening after school and we could not wait to get away when school finished. It was a 20-over match with each bowler restricted to 4 overs. T20 had not yet been invented and we were playing 20 overs because, with the light likely to go, there was no way we could have had a match that lasted more than 40 overs in all. We batted first and I opened the batting. I shall let Omar, who was also playing that evening, take up the story:

The first four overs were strange because Moeen was, I think, a little bit nervous because of the way the Blossomfield guy had given Mo a little bit of mouth when he came to our house. Then Moeen hit him for a four or a six – I cannot remember what it was. After that every bowler that came on just got destroyed. I was padded up and itching to go in but I could only sit and watch this mayhem. No, and I am being absolutely honest, I did not want him to get out. I wanted him to get his 200. A lot of the shots Mo played that evening were just breathtaking to watch. It is nearly twenty years since that evening but that is by far the greatest innings I've seen in cricket.

I missed out on 200 by five runs and in my 195 there were 21 fours and 15 sixes. I cannot now remember what the lad who had tried to play mind games with me said afterwards. What mattered was that Dad was over the moon.

Those two years that I gave my dad of total dedication to cricket made me into a professional cricketer. In those two years we worked day and night. We did a lot of drill work. Dad used to take me everywhere to find a space where I could get a chance to practise batting. It also made me careful about how I behaved at school. At my secondary school I had become a bit more of a rebel, misbehaving and doing things that would be considered naughty. Looking back I wonder why I did what I did at that age. But at the time you have a laugh with your friends and, probably, are at that the stage where your personality is changing. I was suspended multiple times in my first year at Moseley and ended up on report for a couple of years. One infraction was for bad language. Another time my friends and I took stop watches and just threw them in the science lab. Just messed around. After Dad told me to give him two years of my life I had to be careful that I did not get detention. I could not afford to get detention. It would mean no time for the cricket practice Dad had organized.

My school cricket team at Moseley went to the national state school competition, we went to London. We played against Bedford school and King Edward. I used to love it. We were always the underdogs. We didn't have much between us, but we used to just smash the teams and come back. Once we were playing Solihull school who had a couple of county players. We were chasing 130 and we won in 8 overs. We were used to playing on wickets that were not easy to bat on. That was a good pitch and we loved batting on it. I found I could drive with ease. Guys we played with could not afford bats and pads. As a county player I had all the equipment and I used to share all my stuff. When I got out I used to give the pads to the next guy going in. Those are the kind of memories I cherish for ever. We always felt we were going to prove that we were better than them at cricket. When you play you want to beat the opposition. I have always had that mentality. When I am playing against Australia or whoever, and they think they are better, that motivates me to show them that I am better than them.

Dad always believed I could open the batting for England. I remember he once had quite a discussion with Roger Newman, the Warwickshire academy director. Roger used to play with us and take some coaching sessions and he told me, 'You have a flair for hitting the ball hard, Moeen, never lose that flair. Play your shots, wherever you are, whatever level you play go and play your stuff, just tighten up your technique. Don't lose your flair because you won't be the player you are, right?' Roger told Dad, 'Munir, Moeen will play Test cricket for England batting at number six.' Dad immediately responded, 'No, no, no, Roger, he will play number one or two.' But Roger stuck to his views and said, 'In the one-dayers he might open the batting, but in the Test matches he will bat at number six or seven.' That was not a bad prediction.

I often go back to Moseley Ashfield and wander round the lovely olde worlde club house. The pictures on the wall of men in suits speak of a bygone era. It brings back memories and also makes me humble. It makes you realize where you are from. The reason why you play. Sometimes you forget that. My journeys back are a chance to recharge my batteries. The club has now honoured me with my name on the club board with a picture of me playing a flamboyant drive. Underneath it is a sign saying:

Moseley CC Under-11–Under-15. 1998–2002

I	NO	Runs	HS	Hundreds	Average
49	16	1,702	195 n.o.	3	57.58

Overs	Maidens	Runs	Wickets		Average
169	27	518	34		15.24

But one of the pictures I really like is one showing me, Omar, a guy called Walid, one of his best friends and several others. Six of them in the picture played county cricket. I am at the edge of the picture. I look very quiet, very shy, afraid to speak.

For me that innings of 195 was important for it showed me how I can react to provocation or hostile jibes from opponents. I have never believed I should use my tongue to respond when I have a bat. As a kid I never said a lot. I was very shy. I could talk to my teammates about cricket, but what I didn't like, and still don't, was sledging or indulging in verbals with the opposition. I expressed my feelings through my performances on the field.

Yet that innings of 195 would have amounted to nothing had a bush not prevented me from getting killed when I was run over by a mad Asian driver. To this day I do not know what he wanted to do or why. I had left Moseley school early as I had to go for special coaching sessions at Edgbaston. Home was a fifteen-minute walk away and Dad was waiting there to drive me to Edgbaston. As I came out of the main entrance, with my school bag over my shoulder, I saw two girls walking in front, and they were being followed by this Asian guy in a car. The driver said something to one of the girls and the girl said something back. Whatever it was it made him drive faster and then he saw me. Whether he thought I was with the girls or not I don't know but he suddenly reversed his car back and came at me at top speed. I was in shock. The car hit me. Thankfully there was a bush and I fell into it. If there had been a wall it would have been death. It was crazy. I used to be very fair in those days, so did he think I was a white kid? I don't know.

I got up and ran. By this time the car had sped off and turned upside down, although I found that out later. I just wanted to get away. I had been hit in the right leg and was bleeding. There was no way I could get home in that condition. So I went into a corner shop and told the shopkeeper that this guy had tried to run me over and I had to ring home. The shop owner rang Dad and told him I had been in an accident and that I was okay but I had hurt my leg. Dad came as soon as he could and he found me crying. Dad was worried that my leg was broken but he could see it was just bruised and bleeding.

'Moeen, what happened?' Dad asked me.

I said, 'I don't know Dad, this guy ran his car at me. He tried to kill me.'

'Kill you? What do you mean tried to kill you, what did you do?'

'I did nothing,' I insisted. 'I was at school, I was coming home because I am supposed to go to Edgbaston so I left school early.'

'I know,' he said. 'I was waiting for you.'

Dad now said, 'Let's go and have a look at his car.'

By this time Dad had begun to feel funny in his head. That is when we saw the car was upside down. The fire brigade had arrived. The guy was standing next to the car. Dad went up to him and yelled, 'Why did you try and run him over?'

This guy, far from showing any remorse or offering an apology then said the worst thing he could have said: 'He's lucky that I didn't kill him.'

Dad was furious and punched him hard and then hit him again two or three times with his right fist. The police were there interviewing a guy who had come out of his house to find out what the commotion was. The policeman immediately came over to intervene and Dad put him on the spot.

'Officer, if that was your son and if I tried to kill your son for no reason or run him over with my car, you just tell me as a father – what would you have done? Would you have waited and rung the law or what would you have done?'

The policeman said, 'I probably would have done the same as what you did.'

The police took a statement from me. Then he told Dad, 'I've heard what's happened. Take your son home. Look, he's okay, he's got a bit of cut. It's still bleeding. Get him checked over and take him to the hospital.'

The police arrested the man and must have charged him. I don't know. Dad took me home and then to the hospital. I was x-rayed and fortunately there was no break. I didn't need a plaster cast, just a bandage around the leg. Dad then took me to Edgbaston and explained that I'd had an accident. I was bruised but after a few days I was okay.

What took time to get over was the psychological shock. I was very shaken and afraid to come out of the house for a while. It was some time before I recovered and for days after that I did not leave the house except to go to school.

The guy was a local man and a month or so later one evening Dad went to the chip shop and he saw him in the queue buying chips. But he saw Dad and quickly went out without buying anything. Dad was sure he must have recognized him and got scared of what Dad might do. We never saw him again.

I did my best to put this horrific incident behind me and was back at Moseley Ashfield playing as often as I could and enjoying myself. Moseley Ashfield gave me the opportunity to enjoy the game. When I got to the Warwickshire academy it was about tightening my technique, shoring my defence up, which was a problem at that time, and learning how to leave balls that I didn't have to play.

Dad never stopped believing I would play Test cricket. He says that in his lifetime there have been only two Warwickshire boys who he knew, the moment he saw them, would play Test cricket for England. One was Ian Bell who Dad saw as a young lad, technically very good with a very strong head. And the other was me: what impressed Dad was I was never satisfied with 20s and 30s, that I wanted to score 100s all the time. He ranks me with Bell in the way I took on the bowling and was always keen to score runs and score heavily.

But if my batting progressed in a straight line, my bowling changed in the space of four balls I bowled one day at the nets at Edgbaston.

Cricket, like life, is always full of surprises. You never know what is round the corner. Yet what happened that day at Edgbaston nets was so surprising that even now I cannot believe it. My fast-bowling action meant I had developed a bit of backache. Steve Perryman, the bowling coach for Warwickshire at that time who looked after both the junior and the senior teams, was at the nets.

'Steve,' said Dad, 'Moeen has got a bit of a backache, but have you seen him bowl off-spin?'

'No,' said Steve, very surprised. 'Does he bowl off-spin?'

'Yes, I think he has got a very good action. Will you have a look at him'.

So, Steve Perryman gave me a box of six balls and told me to have a bowl, so that he could have a look for himself.

After I had bowled four balls he took the box away and said, 'Moeen, come here, no more seamers. You have got a fairly good action, a strong action.' Then he added words I shall never forget: 'With that sort of action you can go on to play for England.'

You could say I had, in the course of an unfinished over in an indoor net, gone from a teenager who had been told to look at how Glenn McGrath bowls to one who was told to see whether he could become the next Shane Warne.

The two years of intense cricket with my Dad developed me so much that I was the youngest to play in the Birmingham League. As a fifteen-year-old I signed a professional contract with Warwickshire. I was the youngest ever to sign a professional county contract at Edgbaston. By seventeen I was also playing for the England Under-17 side. That was when on a visit to Pakistan I realized how differently we treat young players in this country to the way Pakistan and India do.

Dad, Kadeer, Omar and I had all travelled to Pakistan for a couple of weeks of cricket. We played at Lahore, Rawalpindi and other centres. In the first match Kadeer scored 139 not out. In Islamabad we played a team called RKL, a first-class outfit that had seven Test players. I got a half-century. But the game I really enjoyed was the one in Aftabad. We played a very good side. We scored 245 in 35 or 40 overs. I opened the batting, by the 19th over I was 120 not out. Then the umpire gave me run out. I was in. I looked at him and he said, 'Mafi kar Yar. [Please forgive me.] Go. They want to watch someone else. You have done enough.' The coach said to Dad, 'In one year both your sons will be on the Pakistan circuit.' Dad said, 'No, no. They are going to be playing for England.' Dad was sure that if Kadeer and I were given the chance we would make it.

What we didn't know was that it would take another decade for me to make my England debut. By the time I was hitting my stride as an England cricketer I was thirty, an age when many subcontinent cricketers think of retiring. Sachin Tendulkar was, of course, unique in making his Test debut aged only sixteen. But many other players in the subcontinent play their first Test in their early twenties. My hero Saeed Anwar made his Test debut aged twenty-two, retiring just eleven years later. In Pakistan they believe if you are good enough you should be given the chance to play at the highest level. Age does not matter. We in England feel you have to be mature before you can be risked in the national team. I believe this means many talented players do not get a chance and their promise is not fulfilled.

There is also a South Asian dimension to this that cannot be ignored. Less than 5 per cent of the British population is of South Asian ethnicity, yet 30 per cent play recreational cricket. But look at the first-class game and the figure is only 4 per cent. The ECB is concerned and has spoken about providing 'unconscious bias awareness training' to get more South Asians into the first-class game. The editor of *Wisden*, Lawrence Booth, in his notes for the 2018 edition wrote, 'Unpack the jargon and there is an overdue acknowledgement that Britain's South Asian cricketers have not always been made to feel welcome. That's putting it generously.'

I could not agree more. Young South Asian talent is not nurtured. Many, I am convinced, drop out when they find doors closed even when they are playing well at junior cricket. I was lucky with my dad. Many South Asian families do not have such luck. While 'unconscious bias' training is not a bad thing, what we need is a fundamental change in attitude to ensure that young talent is rewarded and rewarded early and not allowed to lose interest in the game. This is all the more important for talented South Asian cricketers as they have to battle to open two doors. The first door is the family one where the mantra is study, study, study, cricket and sport will get you nowhere. But when they have opened this door and demonstrated how talented they are there is another obstacle: professional cricket can often take so long to recognize their talent that by then they have already given up the sport. There are signs that this is changing just a little but the ECB has a challenge and I wish them well. It is not easy to change a cricket culture which asks how old you are when the question must be how good you are. If you are good enough you are old enough to play cricket as any number of cricketers from India and Pakistan have shown. It is high time we in England followed that example.

CHAPTER 4

NOT WELCOME AT HOME

Me as a baby. I apparently fell off the chair just after this photo was taken!

My younger brother Omar on the left and me on the right. Omar's pulling a classic Asian pose from back in the day.

Me with my siblings – Kadeer on the left, Omar on the right and Azba behind me.

My dad in his playing days. I don't often tell him this but I do love listening to his stories.

The lovely Betty Cox, my grandmother, who taught me so much and has a special place in my heart.

One of my childhood nicknames was Frankenstein, due to the shape and size of my head.

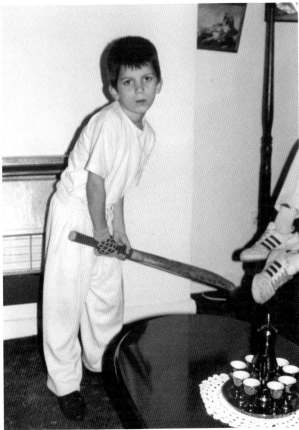

Practising indoors in our old house in Sparkhill.

A school photo, and the first time I had my hair cut very short. Everyone started laughing when I went up to have my photo taken.

Moseley Ashfield days. My pads were always too big!

The Moseley Ashfield Under 13s team of 1999. I'm on the far right of the middle row and Omar is sitting in front of me.

BATSMEN	TIME IN	OUT	MINS AT WKT	RUNS SCORED	SCORE RATE 50	100	HOW OUT	BOWLER	TOTAL
1 M. MUNIR				4446 446 4411 264161424 1666 4246 4616144614 4441646124611161 : 21×4 . 15×6			NOT	OUT	195
2 V. BUTT							LBW	ZIZHAN	0
3 H. LAW				4411			C+B	LEWIS	10
4 A. MAZHAR				116 111			RUN	OUT	11
5 Q. SHAH				6			BOWLED	BOYCE	6
6 J FOURACRE				11111			NOT	OUT	5
7 Z. ALI									
8 A. CLARKE									
9 C. CORFIELD				DID NOT BAT					
10 C. LAW									
11 O. MUNIR									

MOSELEY ASHFIELD U 15×1 CRICKET CLUB V BLOSSOMFIELD U15×1 ....C.CLUB
HOME CLUB ONLY INNINGS OF ... MOSELEY ASHFIELD ... PLAYED AT ... ASHFIELD ... ON FRIDAY 22 JUNE 192001

NOTE Batsmen RUN OUT, or given out for OBSTRUCTION, HIT BALL TWICE, HANDLED BALL do NOT count as bowlers wickets

	NO BALLS			
TOTAL AT THE FALL OF EACH WICKET AND NO. OF OUTGOING BATSMAN	WIDES 1111		4	EXTRAS 9

1 FOR	2 FOR	3 FOR	4 FOR	5 FOR	6 FOR	7 FOR	8 FOR	9 FOR	10 FOR	BOWLING EXTRAS		TOTAL 236
14	55	143	169							BYES 111	3	
2	3	4	5							LEG BYES 11	2	........FOR 4 WKTS.

FIELDING EXTRAS

COPYRIGHT W. BOURNE & CO. LTD, LONDON

The scorecard from my innings of 195 not out for Moseley Ashfield – Omar (batting at no. 11) and I used our middle name 'Munir' as our surname at the time.

Representing the Midlands region at the Lords Taverners Under-14 Festival in 2001. I'm sitting down on the left, and future England goalkeeper Joe Hart is standing, third player from the right.

Aged 16, this is the official photo for my second year at Warwickshire.

One of my favourite photos: my cousin Kabir, my brother Kadeer and me, in a rare game we all played in. It was Worcestershire vs Gloucestershire and Kabir got Kadeer out.

My second year at Worcestershire, which quickly felt like home. Celebrating with Gareth Batty after taking a catch.

Receiving the PCA Player of the Year award in 2013. I was really nervous but it ended up being a great night.

Opening the batting in my first ever game for England (with a fractured thumb).

am a Sparkhill boy and proud of it. Nothing would have given me greater pleasure than to become the cricket equivalent of my football hero Steven Gerrard who, for all José Mourinho's efforts to tempt him to Chelsea, stayed loyal to Liverpool. But it was not to be. I had to leave Warwickshire and it was not by choice.

Right from the beginning the people who ran cricket at Warwickshire made me and my family feel very unwelcome. It has changed now for my dad and Kadeer but what happened when I first started at Edgbaston needs to be recorded to illustrate the problems I faced and why a Warwickshire boy became a Worcestershire man. I had never before encountered such negative vibes. Until then my dad in particular but also Trevor and many others had encouraged me, made me believe in my abilities, assured me that I could aim for the heights. Yet Warwickshire always wanted to make me feel like the outsider who might never make it.

I started my first-class career with my home county in the summer of 2005 with great hope. I had spent January and February, aged sixteen, touring with the England Under-19 team which I'd been selected for on the back of playing a trial game against Bangladesh alongside Stuart Broad, in those days a batsman who didn't bowl. Without meaning to big myself up, by this time I knew I was one of the better players in my age group so while it was a nice surprise to be selected for the national youth squad, at the same time it felt like a natural progression. I was used to playing with men rather than boys and was consistently performing quite well. It was so exciting, a moment of firsts for me. This was my first England tour, the first time I had kit with my name on the back and the three lions of England on my chest. The first time I had got on a plane, the first time I was leaving England to go to places I had read about but never visited. We played two games in Kuala Lumpur, Malaysia, and then went on to India where we played Under-19 Test matches. This was my first trip to India and it showed me how cricket was being taken to far-flung parts of their country. So while two of our Test matches were at historic test centres, in Kolkata and Bengaluru, we also had Tests in the Keenan Stadium in Jamshedpur, the home ground of M. S. Dhoni, although then he was not much known outside his home state of Jharkhand. Our last international was in Siliguri, at a ground charmingly called Kanchanjunga, evoking the great Himalayan mountain of that name and both a cricket and football stadium. Given Indian passion for the Premier League my beloved Liverpool would have packed the 40,000-seater stadium, though we didn't quite draw that number when we played there.

By 2005 India were a cricketing powerhouse – because they had such huge audiences for the game, the sponsorship money was going through the roof. I had an idea of what to expect because Kadeer had spent time there but nothing could have prepared me for the poverty, which make me realize how lucky we are in England and how much we are looked after. The contrast between conditions on the streets and the money that was flowing into Indian cricket couldn't have been greater. But if Indians were lavishing money on development of the game at the grass-roots level, what struck me was their training regime was so much better than ours. They trained a lot more and did not tie down their junior players. In India I saw their net bowlers always bowling, which was not a thing we did, or do today, at that age group. We are always putting restrictions on how many overs you can bowl; the number of overs seamers can bowl is decided by how old you are. So a fifteen-year-old seamer can bowl only 5 overs at a time. That was one of the reasons why I so eagerly accepted Steve Perryman's advice to switch to becoming an off-spinner, as it meant I could bowl a lot more. Indians do not have such restrictions. They believe that if you are good enough your age should not limit your chances to show what you can do.

This may explain why nearly all the Indian players who we played against in their Under-19 side went on to have major international careers for the senior Indian teams while no one apart from me in that Under-19 side went on to Test cricket for England, and it took me a lot longer than the Indians. A few of my teammates played one-day internationals and some, like the captain Steve Davies, Joe Denly and Steve Mullaney, play county cricket. In India it is made easier for young players to mature into international players, as they see the Under-19 side as the springboard for their future Test teams. So we played against Robin Uthappa, S. Dhawan, Ambati Rayudu and Piyush Chawla, all of whom have since become Indian international players. The star was undoubtedly seventeen-year-old Cheteshwar Pujara, who not only scored the Test series' first century in Jamshedpur but made it a double, 211, in a mammoth Indian score of 472 for 4 declared. It was an early indication of a player who once in always makes sure he goes on to score heavily. That was the only Test when I got a chance to turn my arm and had the satisfaction of bowling Pujara's partner, Tiwari, who made 109. As a team we performed poorly with India winning all three Tests and the one-day internationals 4-1.

I began the tour well, steering England to a five-wicket victory against Karnataka at the Chinnaswamy Stadium in Bangalore with 86 not out. In the three Tests I batted I came in at six or seven. The innings that gave me the greatest pleasure was making 41 at Eden Gardens, a ground I had heard so much about. Kolkata was also the place where I had the best biryani I have ever had and to eat the street food of India – in particular Nizam's kathi kabab – was great fun. So while my first tour was challenging on a playing level, it was a great experience all round and I was fascinated by my first taste of India.

*

On a personal level this was a difficult time for me. I was like any sixteen-year-old going to parties until three or four in the morning then playing the next day. I was hanging out with older people and doing things I shouldn't have been doing even though I knew my behaviour was wrong – not in terms of my career, but wrong for my culture and my religion. I did not realize it then but my life was about to change as I searched for the meaning of why we are on this earth although, as I shall narrate, it would be another two years before I would find the serenity, calmness and purpose that has guided me since. I was in the middle of this search when I made my Warwickshire debut against Cambridge University at Fenners on a cold May morning in 2005.

As a seventeen-year-old, playing for my home county was very exciting. Cambridge put us in but I spent the first day watching the rain come down, and there were only 6 overs bowled. On the second day, batting number six, I felt it would be a long time before I would be required to pad up. But Warwickshire were in soon in trouble, losing four wickets for 48. Jonathan Trott was still there and I helped him put on 184 for the fifth wicket. Trotty remained not out on 150 and I made 57, before being caught behind. Unlike my batting for Moseley, I did not smash the bowling, I left that to Trotty, but the innings pleased me and I contributed to our decent first-innings score of 296, which was enough to give us a victory by 18 runs. I did not expect bouquets at the end of the match but nor did I expect the put-down I received from the Warwickshire coach, John

Inverarity, the former Australian player. Instead of encouraging me he gave me what I call the half treatment, a cricket version of school reports which say 'little Johnny could do better'. The only charitable explanation I can give is that he was trying to say I should try harder and become even better. But it was so very different to how Dad encouraged my cricket. I know matches against Cambridge and Oxford do not have the cachet they once had yet I was disappointed that I did not get another chance to play for the first team, let alone make my championship debut.

There was, though, my Under-19 debut for England against Sri Lanka, who had stepped in after Australia decided to restructure their Under-19 cricket. Our performance restored some pride after the winter mauling by the Indians. It gave me an opportunity to play with Stuart Broad who was devastating in the two one-day internationals, both of which we won easily. Our margins of victory, by eight wickets and seven, meant I did not get a chance to bat. But in the first Test at Shenley I managed to get a bat. Coming in at number six with the score 133 for 4, I decided I would attack from the first ball and scored 74 from 85 balls. Our score of 411 was always going to be a challenge for the Sri Lankans and with Broady showing for the first time how he could run through teams, grabbing 5 for 17 in the second innings, we won in a canter. We won the second Test just as easily.

The third Test at Leeds was the one that gave me the most pleasure. In the way that has been a feature of my cricket, higher up the order in one match, down the order the next, I had been demoted to number seven and found myself at the crease in a classic England middle-order stutter, three wickets falling for two runs. My 52 not out, batting with the tail, ensured we made 298. In the previous two Tests I had not bowled much but now I was brought on when the Sri Lankan lower order looked as if it might cause us problems. But in a spell that I felt showed I was not just a batsman who bowled, I took the last four Sri Lankan wickets for 29 runs. I felt like a real off-spinner with a short-leg in position and two of the wickets were Sri Lankan batsmen misreading the spin and getting caught there. This gave us a very handy lead of 143. I was promoted to six in the second innings and came in to bat at the end of the second day's play. When the final day began I didn't need to be told we needed runs quickly and from the first ball went about hitting everything I could. I got to my century in 56 balls. Varun Chopra declared immediately. We did not expect Sri Lanka, set a target of 510, to delay us. But their captain Angelo Mathews made a century, putting on 100 for the ninth wicket and with the clock running it did make us wonder if we might just miss out. I had already taken two wickets, I was brought back on and while I could not get Mathews out I got the last man caught by our captain. *Wisden* would later call it a 'magnificent all round performance'. It helped that Rod Marsh, the ECB academy director, came to every match, encouraged us and kept telling us that we must 'respect the game'.

Four months later we set off for the subcontinent in great heart, this time to Bangladesh, another country new to me and one with which I would soon form a close personal association. We not only played the hosts but also Sri Lanka in a tri-nation tournament. This was another overseas tour where I first met players who would shine for their country, this time Tamin Iqbal and Mushfiqur Rahman for Bangladesh. I began well, scoring 72 in the first match. But the Bogra district stadium was a world removed from Leeds. We lost that match by 28 runs and after that the tour went so disastrously that we lost all eleven matches we played in Bangladesh. The wheels really came off that tour. My only consolation was scoring 70 in the opening tri-nations tournament in another losing cause.

Clearly something needed to change as we headed to Sri Lanka for the Under-19 World Cup. But while the cricket was dreadful my life was changing. I was no longer the party animal searching for meaning that I had been on my previous visit to the subcontinent. I had begun to grow a beard. I had not yet found all the answers I was looking for, but I felt confident in myself. Not long after we had lost our eleventh and last match, Andy Pick, the Under-19 coach, summoned me and we talked team tactics. I made the point that we had played mostly spin – Bangladesh and Sri Lankan spinners had bowled 40 of the 50 overs we faced – and we had not played spin bowling cleverly. Our batters always wanted to play the spinners square off the wicket when there was not enough pace on the ball and we'd also rarely succeeded when trying to sweep. My analysis seemed to impress Pick and he decided that I would take over from Varun Chopra as captain for the

Under-19 World Cup. He told me that that Varun would now play under me but felt I was very mature and that from a kid I had become a man and could handle the pressure of having the ex-captain in the dressing room.

My start as captain could not have been better. I have always seen myself as a top-order batsman, so in our first Under-19 World Cup match in Group D against Nepal at the Sinhalese Sports Cub in Colombo on 6 February 2006, I decided I would bat number four, making 54 in 82 minutes from 82 balls, hitting three fours and two sixes in our score of 209 for 9 in 50 overs. Our spinners made sure Nepal were all out for 132 in 45.2 overs. It was very pleasing to be made Player of the Match. Two days later we moved to another ground in Colombo, the Colombo Cricket Club, and had a much more difficult match against Ireland, winning by just four runs, and so qualified for the quarter-finals. The final group match, in yet another ground in Colombo, was again another close-run thing against Zimbabwe and this was a very new experience. So far in my Under-19 career I had faced players who were seen as future stars of their countries. Now I was up against a player who, on my Test debut at Lord's, I was to partner if only for a brief period as he steered England to a winning position. That was our very own 'Gazza', Gary Ballance. Born in Harare five months after I arrived on that trolley in Birmingham, he was then playing for the land of his birth. That day I had Gazza stumped for 47 but he showed his class. It was enough to make him Player of the Match and Zimbabwe winners by two wickets.

In the quarter-finals nobody gave us any chance to win as we faced Bangladesh, bringing back memories of our pre-Christmas tour. Bangladesh had also beaten a strong Pakistan side. But we bowled out Bangladesh for 155 in 48.2 overs and then Varun played a marvellous innings to be Player of the Match. Now in the last four we had to take on the formidable Indians. Could we spring another surprise?

Sadly it wasn't to be. The semi-final on 15 February, again in Colombo, ended in a heavy defeat. The Indians batted first and made 292 for 4 in 50 overs with Pujara making 129 not out and for the first time our quartet of spinners, Graeme White, Nick James, Rory Hamilton-Brown and myself, could not tie down the batsmen. Worse still, when we batted we made only 58 in 20.1 overs with only one batsman, Graeme White, making double figures. I made just 4. In the final it was India's turn to collapse for 71, losing a match they looked like they had won when they bowled out Pakistan for 109. But while all this summed up the unpredictability of Under-19 cricket I returned home feeling confident and happy. I was working out a pattern for my life and felt good about my cricket.

My new contentment was soon dispelled when a cricketing drama at Warwickshire began to unfold which by the end of 2006 season meant I could no longer play for my home county. It centred round the way the club continued to treat my family with this time Omar the subject of their wrath. He had started well. He often showed his class. In one match as a fifteen-year-old playing with Chris Woakes in an Under-17 two-day match, at Warmley against Cheshire, Omar came in when we had lost three wickets for five runs and he made an unbeaten double hundred. In another game he got 80-odd against Lancashire, and there were other good performances too. Yet they were not enough to impress Mark Greatbatch, the former New Zealand batsman who had taken over as cricket academy coach. The problem as he saw it was Dad. On the face of it Dad was well-established: he had qualified as a coach and had an indoor centre at Edgbaston. But he had blotted his copybook because of the way he had taken Kabir and Kadeer away from Warwickshire.

My cousin Kabir had been offered a scholarship by Worcester. Dad and Chacha Shabir took him and Kadeer to the Evesham indoor centre and they both impressed Worcester's coaches. They wanted to sign Kabir but did not have the money to sign Kadeer as well. Chacha Shabir suggested that we would be willing to share the scholarship and Worcester agreed, saying this was a matter for the Ali family. Dad came back to Edgbaston and told them that they hadn't given Kabir the opportunity he deserved. But now, seeing this interest from Worcester, they suddenly offered Kabir a three-year contract. Dad's response was pointed: 'Only two days ago you had said to me he wasn't good enough, he wasn't ready,' he said. 'Now that there is an approach from another county all of a sudden he is ready.' Dad also spoke to Warwickshire about Kadeer and they told him that they could do nothing about him as he was only fifteen.

Dad and Chacha Shabir decided that with Worcester offering both Kabir and Kadeer a scholarship they would move. They had invested so much in our cricket and this was the first time our family was actually going to make an income from it.

This row put the authorities at Warwickshire on alert and Dad was marked down as 'Munir the troublemaker'. Whispers reached him that people at Edgbaston were saying, 'Oh, Munir is demanding and Munir wants this and he wants that for his boys.' Dad's view had always been if the boys were good enough then he wanted the recognition. If they weren't good enough, fair enough. If they hadn't scored runs or if they hadn't fulfilled their talent then not giving them chances was fine.

For Dad Warwickshire's attitude to Omar was illustrated when there was an awards night for the boys from the academy. Held in one of the big conference rooms at Edgbaston, Dad took Omar there hoping he might get an award. Not only did he not get one, but no mention was made of his 200 not out, the highest score anybody had scored in Warwickshire youth cricket ranging from Under-10s to Under-19s. Some of the parents came up to Dad and said how they felt it was a shame Omar was not even mentioned. Omar came away crestfallen.

Warwickshire seemed to cut Omar no slack. One week the boys were supposed to do fitness training. Simon Holyhead was the fitness coach. Omar was called to Loughborough with the England Under-17 squad, so he went there and was marked down by Warwickshire as absent. Dad protested and asked them to contact John Abrahams, who was in charge at

Loughborough England Under-17s. But they didn't. You cannot blame Dad for feeling that he was the most hated person at Edgbaston.

It was after this that Greatbatch called Dad in for a meeting about Omar's future. Without getting to know Dad, or really talking to him, he announced, 'We've decided not to take Omar in the academy this year.' Omar had been averaging 30 when his team mates were averaging 14 and 15. Dad was surprised but Greatbatch's mind was made up. Dad says:

I got the impression that Greatbatch's mind had been filled with all the anti-Munir stuff then swirling round Edgbaston. Warwickshire felt that I needed to be put in my place and the way to do that was kick Omar out. All I was doing was fighting for the rights of my boys. Any dad would do that. Maybe other fathers didn't have the guts. They did not have the courage to go and talk to somebody. I feel that I was brave enough to go and talk. So when in that meeting Mark Greatbatch said we can offer Omar a Development of Excellence I said, 'Well, I don't want a DoE; he was in the academy last year.' If he had performed badly in the academy that was something else. But he had done well. He was in the England Under-17 set-up; he was only fifteen then.

I had gone into this meeting thinking Greatbatch was a former Test player, a great person. But on hearing what he said I thought I don't need to listen to this rubbish. I honestly thought, Oh bloody hell, what a person. If Omar had not performed, I would have said 'yes' and put my hand up. I didn't want a contract for Omar in the way Moeen had got one at fifteen. I just wanted him to be where he was in the academy, given the opportunity. It was clear to me they had kicked Omar out because of me. I told Greatbatch, 'I don't want your DoE.... Keep the DoE.' I walked out, but in my mind I said, 'Okay, that's fine, you know my name is Munir and you know I'm not an easy guy to deal with. I'll get even. I'm going to fight fire with fire. I have the ace card in my hand.'

The ace in the hand he was referring to was me. For I was in the last season of my contract and would have to decide whether I should continue with Warwickshire when the 2006 season ended.

Dad told me the story after he got home. I was shocked at the club's attitude and I said, 'Dad, you're right.' I could see Dad was fuming. 'You calm down; you'll win.'

I was soon to get to know Greatbatch and see first-hand how he could put people's backs up. He just didn't seem to know how to be a good coach, particularly when it came to dealing with young players. The end of the 2005 season had seen some turmoil in Warwickshire. Nick Knight gave up the captaincy with Heath Streak taking over – Warwickshire's seventh captain in eleven seasons. Inverarity went back to Australia. That is when the county decided that the coach for the 2006 season would be Greatbatch.

From the beginning of the season I found him very difficult to trust. He was very inconsistent in his ways. For example, I would get picked but wouldn't bat or bowl in the whole game. The next game I was dropped.

I made my county debut at Trent Bridge on 3 May. Nottinghamshire won the toss, put us in and I came into bat at 133 for 6. As often happens on Broady's home ground, the conditions helped swing and seam but as the sun came out I could bat more freely. At the end of the first day I was 68 not out and thought I might score a century on my debut. The second morning I nicked Ryan Sidebottom to Notts keeper David Alleyne without adding to my score but I had every reason to feel pleased. Many years earlier I had played the Nottinghamshire second team at Trent Bridge, and made 50-odd. Steve Perryman had told my dad, 'Many years ago, I saw a player, a left-hander, very elegant, and I was very impressed and today I saw another player which reminded me of that player and I think he's going to go far.' My dad asked him who the player was that he was comparing me with and he said, 'David Gower.' How flattering it was that when *Wisden* wrote the match report they said, 'Elegant and free-flowing, Ali evoked comparisons with David Gower, and a 68 looked even more valuable next day, as Warwickshire's seamers dominated.' We won by 60 runs.

But it made no impression on Greatbatch. I expected the coach to have some words of praise for me. Instead he said, 'Don't expect to get picked. Don't think you will be in the team,

You will be in and out for the next five years.' When I told Dad he exploded. 'Five years!' he said. 'Warwickshire is a big county. I know they have a lot of players and there is a lot more competition here. But in the team, out of the team is not a way to encourage youngsters. It is not how old you are, Moeen. It is how good you are.'

Three days after this victory, when Warwickshire returned home to play Hampshire, there was no Ali in the side. David Gower one day. Nonentity the next. Hampshire had Shane Warne and I so wanted to play against him. It was mid-June before I made my home debut against Lancashire batting number eight; getting a chance to bowl, I took two Lancashire wickets. I kept popping in and out of the side. My fourth county match was in the last week of August against Durham at Chester-le-Street. Now I was promoted to number three. Wickets clattered all around me as Durham's pace attack bowled devastatingly. I made 68 again and although we lost the match, young players need to be boosted not put down. But Greatbatch was different. By now I was finding him very difficult to work with. His demeanour was often sullen, giving the impression that it was an effort to talk to you. For a young player this was forbidding. He had a reputation for being a strong, hard-nosed coach. I felt I saw straight through him. I just did not want to play under him at that time. The crunch moment when he dropped me for a lad called Nick James, my age, despite the fact that when given the chance in 40-overs cricket I did really well. There was one Sunday match against Durham at Edgbaston which I felt very happy about.

The wicket had been used for a match the previous week and had been treated with glue. We were chasing 213. Graham Onions was much in the news having just been called up for the one-day squad against Pakistan. He was on fire, taking two wickets for two runs in the first two overs, including Nick Knight, who had opened the batting. Trotty, who had come in number three, was at the other end and resolved to hunker down. I decided we must hit our way out of trouble. In 35 balls I hit 57 with two sixes and eight fours. I eventually got caught in the covers. But that didn't worry me. In such situations I have always believed you have got to take on the bowlers. You cannot allow them to dictate. Maybe this approach did not suit Greatbatch.

At home Dad and I often discussed my problems with Greatbatch. 'Dad, it's not going to be easy for me to break into the team yet.' Dad reassured me saying, 'If you are doing well they must play you. Just keep scoring runs.' But having had his problems over Kabir and Kadeer and with getting me my contract, he knew how difficult Warwickshire could be and laid his plans.

The decisive move was made when I was playing in a second XI match against Worcestershire at Ombersley, a nice little ground in a beautiful setting with a lovely pavilion and outside benches and chairs. It has a nice pacy wicket and I was batting at the time when Dad, who knew the people at Worcester, asked Damon D'Oliveira, the second-team coach, if they were looking to sign anybody for next year.

'We have got enough,' replied Damon. 'But we will sign only if Moeen is coming.

Dad said, 'Well, you never know, Moeen might be available.'

He and Uncle Shabir, who was also there, then walked round the ground watching me bat. They had brought a picnic and were enjoying the game when about an hour later Worcester head coach Steve Rhodes arrived. Obviously Damon must have tipped him off. D'Oliveira and Rhodes made it clear to Dad they would like to sign me. Dad said, 'Moeen is in the last year of his contract. I have got a few problems at Warwickshire. I'll go back and I'll talk and I'll think about it.' They left it at that, expecting Dad to come back. Dad also spoke to Nottinghamshire but Worcester, where Kadeer had played – he had by now moved to Gloucestershire – and where Kabir was still playing, was the more obvious choice.

The meeting at Ombersley was followed by another at Worcester when Dad talked at length with Rhodes. Steve promised him that I would be treated very differently to the way I was being treated now. They had six batsmen led by Graeme Hick and captain Vikram Solanki, also Mitchell, Moore, Smith and Davies and I would be the seventh one. I would start off in the second XI but if I did well or there was an injury I would be in the first team. If I did enough to justify my slot I would stay there. Another attraction for me was that Kabir was opening the bowling so it would be quite a family reunion.

Dad also had a chat with Dennis Amiss, who had brought Greatbatch in. As Warwickshire chief executive he knew about the problems with Greatbatch and had heard rumours that I might be about to leave. Amiss set about trying to convince Dad that I should stay at Warwickshire. But Dad never felt comfortable at these meetings. He always felt that at Warwickshire he had this bad guy image. The word round the power brokers of the county was that Munir Ali would hold a knife to Warwickshire's throat to get deals for his sons, when all we were asking for was fair treatment.

It was mid-September when Dad finally decided the move to Worcestershire would be for the best. His great worry was that if I committed myself again to Warwickshire and things continued to go wrong I would not have a leg to stand on. I needed a fresh start, away from all the tensions and troubles.

When Dad initially told me he wanted me to sign for Worcestershire I had some mixed feelings. I was not happy leaving my home county because that is where I was brought up. But I needed to be playing in the first XI. As I reflected I thought that not only was Greatbatch a problem but Heath's leadership could also be very inconsistent: one moment very inspired, but too often inert. This was no way to foster team spirit. I was also not enjoying the atmosphere round the dressing room. Everyone in there was so competitive but in a negative, destructive sense. The atmosphere was such that a player who was replaced by another player was willing his replacement to do badly and fail. It was a dog-eat-dog environment. When you spend a lot time with people like that you end up becoming like them. It is always me, me, me. I didn't like that about myself.

Naturally the atmosphere in the dressing room was much discussed by the younger players. At that time we youngsters were all competing for one or two spots. There was Nick Tarrant and couple of younger guys like Naideep Prunier and Luke Parker. As it happened they ended up staying and, sad as I was to leave, I knew Dad was right. If I was to fulfil my dream of playing for England, much as I loved Warwickshire and would never dream of living anywhere else, I had to find another place for my work. I just couldn't see myself getting the opportunities at Edgbaston. I now had to reconcile myself to making the drive to the New Road ground that Kadeer and Kabir had been making for so long.

There were continued murmurings from disgruntled senior players but in the end the threatened revolt never materialized. Warwickshire carried on with Greatbatch, although 2007 proved a disaster with the county suffering a double relegation from the county championship and the NatWest Pro 40 League.

Warwickshire did come back and make me an offer but by then Dad had given his word to Worcestershire and there was no going back. At the end of the season, when Greatbatch heard I was leaving he told me that I was pencilled in for the first team. I didn't trust him. Being pencilled in was no good to me. I wanted to be in the team as a regular and that was what Worcester offered.

Dad and I drove down to New Road and they simply said 'welcome' and were very happy to sign me. I was absolutely delighted. Steve Rhodes was there, Damon D'Oliveira, the club president John Chadd and chief executive Mark Newton. I think they were very pleased by now that Kabir was there anyway, and now they had Moeen.

So I left my home county thinking the really memorable part of the summer was not the cricket but what happened in my fifth and last first-class match for Warwickshire at Blackpool against Lancashire at the end of August. Play was halted twice by water bombs catapulted onto the pitch from outside the ground. One of them landed very near the Indian Test player Murali Kartik. I can still remember one of the Lancashire cricketers, Mal Loye, scaling the wall dividing the ground from the rest of Stanley Park and giving chase to find the boys who had done this while stewards scanned the Italian garden. When four teenagers were seen cycling towards Blackpool Zoo, somebody joked that they hoped they would be devoured by lions. The groundsmen had to use a bar towel to dry the pitch before we could restart.

But for me the most important match of the summer was one played earlier that month at Edgbaston. The match itself was unremarkable. You would have to search *Wisden* to find anything about it and it did nothing for my cricketing career. But during the course of that match I met a man who was to have a dramatic impact on my life. My move to Worcestershire at the end of September transformed my cricketing fortunes but that meeting in early August 2006 transformed my life. I was leaving my cricketing home because they had not made me welcome.

One of the other reasons I left Warwickshire was that changes were going on in my life. But now, at the headquarters of the home county I was about to leave, I found the spiritual centre that I had been seeking for so many years.

CHAPTER 5

THE DAY IT ALL MADE SENSE

It was very cold and rainy in Birmingham on 2 August 2006. Not an ideal day for cricket. The sort of day you would want to be indoors. I was at Edgbaston playing for Warwickshire against the West Indies A team touring England. It rained most of the day, we managed only a few overs and that afternoon I was sitting by the dressing-room window looking at the rain falling. There were very few people there despite the fact that admission was free. Then, as I looked out of the window, I saw a man make salaams to me. He had a beard and looking at him I was certain he was a Muslim and yet he looked West Indian. This is very unusual, I thought. Surely he must have converted to Islam. I wanted to find out more about him. My desire to meet him was all the greater because I was in the middle of a long search to find myself.

Ever since the age of sixteen I had been searching answers for the purpose of life. Why were we here on earth? Who has created us? Is there a reason for our existence? Where do we go from here? These were the questions I kept asking myself. In my search for the truth I had read many books, gone through philosophies and religions, Hinduism, Christianity, Judaism,

Buddhism. At this stage actually Islam was the one religion I was almost slightly against. I didn't agree with a lot of things which I thought were part of the religion, for example arranged marriages. My family had never been particularly devout. Dad went to the mosque for zumma prayers every Friday, while my mother always used to tell me to pray and would take me to the mosque with her, but that was the extent of it.

At this stage in my life my search for truth meant I had lost touch with my best friends from school, the six or seven of us who used to hang around together. Growing up I was always with them and I would talk to them for hours. Now I wanted no distractions as I tried to make sense of life and strengthen the self-belief welling up inside me. If I had a day off I would literally spend my whole day in the mosque. Just sitting there, reading, talking, praying. After I had prayed once I would wait in the mosque for the next prayer. It was almost like I was secluding myself from everyone, just to build up and maintain this inner peace as long as I could. Inner peace I felt was so important in my life.

The Islam that my family followed had a lot of practices which I had been told were fundamental to the faith. When I started reading the Koran in translation, I began to question some of those practices. So, for instance, like all my family members, I wore a chain round my neck called the Taviz. It was supposed to contain verses of the Koran and was worn to protect you as a lucky charm. One day I had gone to the mosque to pray and as I was coming out, an Arab was going into the mosque. We started talking as you do, and he said, 'What is that around your neck?'

I said, 'That is a Taviz.' I am sure he knew exactly what it was, he was just asking to test me.

He said, 'What does it do, what is in it?'

I said my grandfather had given it to me, it is for protection, it's got the verses of the Koran in it.

'It is Allah who protects you,' he replied. That made me think straight away, You know, he is right.

The other thing he said was, 'Do you go to the toilet?'

'Yes, of course.'

'Do you take the verses of the Koran to the toilet?' he asked. 'Because obviously it is such a holy book you wouldn't take it to the toilet.'

That really made me sit up. I took off the Taviz and opened it up. It was empty. I was later to learn that such amulets sometimes contained numbers. None of them had verses from the Koran. I decided I was not going to wear a Taviz. It didn't make sense.

I noticed that the West Indian was not wearing a Taviz. I decided I was going to go to this guy and ask him a few questions.

I took some apples and oranges – there are always some in the fruit bowl in the dressing room – put them in a tissue and went to where he was sitting huddled up against the cold and rain. I opened the tissue and said, 'Brother take some.' He salaamed and I said, 'Salam alaikum' (peace be upon you) and then I asked him, 'Are you Muslim?' He said he was and that he was a convert. I asked him why he became a Muslim.

He said, 'Look, sit down,' and we started talking. I introduced myself and he told me his name was Ray Walee and that he worked for the social services. He had come to Edgbaston that day with a friend who knew Joel Garner, who was managing the A team. Garner was one of Walee's heroes. He'd always wanted to meet Garner and during the course of the match he did so.

His parents had come from Jamaica, part of the Windrush generation of the late fifties and sixties. They settled in Birmingham where Walee was born. Like me he was a Brummie lad. I was keen to know his journey, how he had become a Muslim. Walee told me his parents were Pentecostal Christians. His mother was devout and went to church a lot, but his father was a Christian in name only and a heavy drinker. Walee had been baptised. A good friend of his, born in Palestine, became Muslim and initially his reaction was this is an Asian religion, why have you become Muslim, we're Christians. His friend told Walee, no, Islam teaches us about worshipping God. In Islam you believe in treating everybody equally and with respect.

That is when Walee started looking at Islam and it made a lot of sense to him. He realized a lot of the values that his father and mother had instilled in him were very Islamic. Treating people kindly and fairly, checking on your neighbours, having respect for your elders and equally treating the youngsters with respect; just generally good family values. He started studying the faith and after three of years of reading he embraced Islam in 1997.

I asked him about arranged marriages and other cultural things, and he said to me, 'This is not your religion, this is not the religion of Islam, it's not part of Islam.' What is he talking about, I wondered. He said, 'No, this is part of your Pakistani culture.' That really hit home and I said, 'Oh, what?'

I told him my family were Sufis and we had Sufi Pirs, or spiritual guides. He told me that to follow Islam properly I must realize Sufism is a branch of Islam which is not from the original teachings of Islam; it's something which was introduced later on, but it wasn't the original teachings of the prophet Muhammad. This was something I didn't know. As for the Taviz he said that it was a cultural thing, nothing to do with Islam. To wear a Taviz means you're putting your trust in something other than Allah. One of the biggest things in Islam is you attribute everything to God, so for example God is all-seeing, God is all-hearing, and nobody else can be all-seeing, all-hearing. When God says he is the protector, then why do we put our trust in a Taviz? And obviously you wouldn't go into the toilet with verses of the Koran hung around your neck. He mentioned that a lot of people think what they are doing is Islamic but it isn't from the religion, they are cultural things. That was the point he made that really struck me: the need to distinguish between the culture and the religion. A lot of people are having problems with the religion because what they're following is not in the Koran but derived from their culture. Apart from the Taviz the other example he gave was Muslims going to graves and praying, which completely goes against the tenets of Islam.

When Walee had spotted me sitting by the window and seen my beard, he hadn't realized Warwickshire had any Muslim guys.

That is when he decided to give me a salaam. Walee was very surprised that I had come to talk to him. He told me in all his years of watching cricket he had never seen a cricketer playing in a match sit down with a stranger and talk. His experience was that while the match was going on, players would normally come into the crowd, have a quick chat with their mates and run back. To see a player in whites suddenly next to him had come as something of a shock.

I chatted with Walee for fifteen or twenty minutes before I had to go back to the dressing room. He took my number and we agreed to talk on the phone. Just before I left he asked me to wait for a few minutes and ran off towards the car park. He brought back a couple of CDs containing lectures on Islam.

I went back to the match and although our side was a very inexperienced one, with no capped players, we won easily. I only made 5 runs but was brought on to bowl with the West Indies looking like they would make us bat again. Their last-wicket pair had put on 52 and they required another 7 to avoid an innings defeat. With my fifth ball I had the last West Indian batsman Mohammed leg-before and we won by an innings and six runs. But more than the cricket, what I had taken away from the match was meeting the first person who could tell me what Islam was really about.

I spoke to Walee on the phone often, we would meet and have coffee or a bite to eat in a restaurant on Coventry Road, one of Birmingham's most culturally diverse shopping areas. Walee told me about his life. His mother was alive, but his father had passed away in 1997. Walee was a sound engineer by trade, and used to work in the music business for UB40, Simply Red, Cameo and a lot of other rock bands. He travelled a lot, which he said was like going to university, a chance to learn a lot about people and their cultures. He was always accepting of other people's cultures rather than dismissive. He was into football and was a big West Indies cricket fan. Watching them play, he felt that they were representing Caribbean people; they gave West Indians in this country hope, a purpose. When he was growing up and when the great West Indies sides toured England, his dad and his friends would gather in the living room of their house, switch on the television but turn off the sound and tune into Radio 4 to listen to *Test Match Special*. There would be white rum, Jamaican food, Domino's pizzas in between lunch and tea, and the kids had to keep quiet when the cricket was on. He told me how in 1994–95, just as he was reading about Islam, he went to Israel touring with Simply Red and UB40 looking after the instruments; for UB40 he looked after the bass player and all the radio systems. He carried with him a copy of the Koran and the Israeli soldiers began checking him thinking he must be a Muslim because he was carrying a Koran into Israel.

Whenever we met we discussed Islam a lot. About my journey, what I was thinking, the correct path to follow. He would give the proof and the evidence from the textbooks, from the Koran and the Hadiths, the sayings and traditions of the prophet Muhammad. I would throw lots of questions at him, all the controversial ones and he had answers for all of them.

Walee feels strongly that young Muslims are being radical-ized because they don't understand the fundamentals of their religion. He has set up a charity to educate them and regu-larly meets young men released from prison whom he mentors to get them back onto the straight and narrow and help them keep out of trouble.

Walee has told me many times that it is fundamental to Islam that we don't do killing, or disrespect our elders. One of his most important points was that as a Muslim living in a non-Muslim land, you're a guest and there's an agreement with your host country that you have to abide by the law of that land. This is Islam. He then told me that the Prophet sent the early Muslims who were being persecuted to Ethiopia. He told them go to this country and seek refuge there, and that the Ethiopian king was Christian and a just man and Muslims had to adhere to the law of that land. Throughout history we've had Muslims living with Christians, with Jews, with atheists and other non-Muslims, and there has been peace and harmony before. There is a minority in all religions who cause problems and spread hatred but we shouldn't let the human bond between us break, regardless of religion. Muslims always want peace for ourselves, our brothers and sisters and our neighbours, all over the world.

There was one particular book he gave me called *The Prayer of the Traveller*. It told me that in Islam if you travel outside your normal jurisdiction – which we call home – or if, as some of the scholars say, you class the travel as a journey for which you need to pack because of the distance covered, you can shorten your prayers. So basically if this happens Islam accommodates the fact that you're a traveller, and it allows you to shorten your prayers or even to combine your prayers. So the religion makes it easy for you to still practise your faith. This applies to Ramadan where if you're travelling you are excused from fasting.

Although my meeting Walee at Edgbaston when rain stopped play was extraordinary, Walee feels that it was not a surprise. In Islam there is predestination, so it was written that on that August day I was going to meet him.

While Walee talked to me about God and how we should put all our trust in God and taught me all these new things about Islam, I also met Majid. I met him at the indoor cricket school at Saltley leisure centre that Dad ran every Saturday. Majid, a wicketkeeper batsman, was a family friend in his mid-thirties and a very good indoor player. When I first met him he was a normal guy of Pakistani origin who went for Friday prayers. Then I saw a transformation and he began to tell me stories about the Prophet and his companions. As he told me these stories my heart was pounding as if it was coming out of my body. It was such a surreal sensation. I remember feeling and thinking these are such beautiful characteristics, this is how a man should be.

Dad was surprised and he was a bit worried that this man was having an influence on me. I kept reassuring him it was nothing like that. He didn't want me to be too extreme about things; maybe he was worried about it affecting my cricket. I pointed out to him that the Islam our family had practised for generations was a mixture of other cultures. It was not the true Islam. We spoke about the Taviz and I said Prophet Muhammad never wore a Taviz. I also thought a great deal about celebrating the Prophet's birthday.

My family like millions of other Muslims had always celebrated Milad un Nabi which marks the birthday of the Prophet. The event sees public gatherings of Muslims. As well as recounting the Prophet's life, salutations and songs in his praise are recited. In some countries, streets and mosques are decorated and illuminated at night. But as I pointed out to Dad and members of my family, there is no historical evidence that the Prophet celebrated his birthday, so why should we do so?

My views did not always go down well, as I realized when I went to weddings. The summer is a great time for weddings, lavish celebrations spread over many days. Often at these weddings one of my cousins or an uncle would argue with me. I know the fundamentals and basics of Islam and a guiding principle is da'wah, which means informing others about the religion. Our job is to call people to religion whenever there's an opportunity, but importantly, if people don't want to take up the call, you should never hold a grudge. You accept their view as you're not in charge of that person's heart. But I'm not a very controversial guy. If I feel as if somebody is not recognizing the facts or somebody has a differing opinion, fine. I try and make them understand gently, reasonably, that they are wrong but ultimately they will have their own truth. That summer saw many arguments.

It was a huge relief when at one family wedding Kadeer said to me, 'What you are saying is making sense.' I felt for the first time someone was on my side, which gave me a lot of confidence.

But while my immediate family accepted what I was saying, I did have disagreements with members of my wider family. We are unusual in that in our wider family we have a Pir, a religious man. He is a very good scholar and extremely knowledgeable, with millions of followers in Pakistan and India though he's not someone I would choose to follow. People from all over the subcontinent come to him for dua (blessing), touch his feet and give him thousands of pounds. They say, 'I have got a stomach ache; let's go to the Pir sahib.' This is a strand of worship which is not in the Koran or the hadiths but rather reflects the culture of the region and the influence of other religions. In a way it helped that there was a Pir in my family, in that it clarified for me that what the Pir was doing wasn't in the Koran.

The discussions about these matters were often very passionate, and they did sometimes anger me a little. For the first time in my life I knew I was doing something right and people were questioning me. But that actually egged me on to do even more. Go against them, I thought. All this time I felt I had been doing the wrong thing. Now I was doing the right thing. An important part of Islam is getting as much knowledge as you can, not just about religion, and this gathering of knowledge is a solitary pursuit. But at the same time, you mustn't become somebody who thinks he knows everything – sometimes it's wise to say I don't know.

Let Dad talk about what my discovering true Islam did to the family:

Religion made him a better player. Once he became more religious and started to understand Islam and the culture and what it is, he focused better on his cricket and changed from a boy into a man. What it did was it helped him to be calm. Moeen finding true Islam has had a great influence on the family. Moeen has changed the trend in the house. You see my wife used to read the Namaz, I used to like Jumma. We'd go to mosque on a Friday, or Eid day and all that, and occasionally if I was with friends and they went to mosque, I would go too. But I wasn't a follower to be honest, and it was just that when Moeen started to change, the other boys, Kadeer and Omar, changed, and so did my daughter. When Moeen started to research and learn about Islam in more detail, even the family started to realize that in the Islam we had practised the cultural aspect had come before religion. There was a change in that regard in the house, which did cause conflict with my father. Before my father passed away we were talking about religion and I said we don't celebrate the Prophet's birthday. My father was from the old school and he got angry and said, 'Are you telling me that we were wrong and you're right?' I said, 'No, I'm not saying they are wrong, but what I'm saying is they did what they were told by the Mullahs and everything. But now the books are out and we read about what we should and shouldn't do and we are here to change things.' He wasn't very happy with what I was saying. And there were people of our wider family who used to talk about Moeen this and Moeen that. Even in our extended household my uncles and others called Moeen 'Wo Wahhabi'. He is a Wahhabi, while we are actually Sunni.

I know I have been called a Wahhabi. But I am not. I know there are different sects in Islam. But they emerged after the Prophet died. I don't follow any particular sect. My search always is what did the Prophet do? What did the Prophet say? I get questioned a lot by my family about why I've taken the Taviz off, and why I don't celebrate the Prophet's birthday. It took me a while to understand that sharing knowledge is different to debating, and there's no point in having a heated discussion. Differences of opinion are fine in Islam … the crucial thing is that we're all human beings and worthy of respect.

Another crucial part of my faith is charity. One of the pillars of Islam is zakat, the compulsory donation of 2.5% of your annual salary to charity. On top of that, there is sadaqah, which is optional charitable contributions. I find this aspect of the religion incredibly rewarding. You don't give your charity only to Muslims, it's distributed to whoever is in need, regardless of religion. Living the selfish life of a modern sportsman, there's a contentment in my heart when I feel like I'm contributing to the wellbeing of society for a change.

I went on my first Hajj when I was twenty-two and ever since I go to Mecca often. Whenever I have time for a holiday I go to

Mecca. Last summer, the moment the cricket was over I headed out to Mecca. I spent three days in Medina, then three days in Mecca. First and foremost I gave thanks for the amazing year that I had had. I also wanted to ask for forgiveness and refresh myself spiritually in that special place where you emerge much stronger in terms of your faith, your personality, your character.

In many households up and down the country, the trend is very similar in that the generation of the children that are born here in the UK are now starting to educate themselves. We are the third generation to come from Pakistan. We do not have to accept what our ancestors did. I see this more an awakening of the youth here and the new generation. They're looking at Islam and thinking, look at the way we are portrayed in the media. Let's not take what our parents say about our faith and how we pray and what we do, let's actually read the Koran and books that teach us about the Prophet. We've got the intelligence, we've got the knowhow, we study in school, we study in universities, why shouldn't we study our faith? Why do we just accept what was done by the generations that preceded us? That's what has started to happen up and down the land. I hope I am playing my part in spearheading it.

It is a sign of confidence that we can look at our religion. To see what it really is not what it is represented as. The Prophet always said that if you want people to come to Islam you have to show them the good things, the humbleness, the neighbourly things, the things that you should be doing as a norm and then people will come to our religion.

My generation is looking at Islam in a way that allows it to integrate into society here in the UK and that scares a lot of people. It scares a lot of our previous generations and it obviously scares those who don't want us to integrate. And the media are extremely unhelpful. Whenever a Muslim or an Asian person commits a crime, his religion is always held up as part of the problem, whereas if it's a white person, they're usually described as a lone wolf struggling with a mental health issue. Obviously there are extremists in all walks of life, in Christianity, Buddhism, Judaism and those extremists who want Sharia law in England, which goes against the teachings of the Koran.

My marriage illustrates how our generation is different to that of my parents. As I have said, Dad had an arranged marriage and only met my mum on the night of their wedding. I was always convinced I was never going to have an arranged marriage, I was totally against it. My parents, thankfully, were understanding and never once spoke to me about having an arranged marriage.

Once I had committed myself to Islam it felt like the time to get married. Even as a kid, when I was fifteen or sixteen, I wanted to get married young. I don't know why I felt that way. Whatever the reason it was just something that I wanted to do. By the time I was nineteen, I was looking to get married. I met my wife in London through a friend – she was working as a receptionist for an optician. I saw her and I liked her. Her name was Firuza Hussain. I asked her if she was married and the answer was no. We got to know each other by phone just by talking and messaging. We never went on dates and we relied totally on love after marriage. I didn't want to tell my family about Firuza until I'd met her parents, who were Bangladeshi and lived in Bow. The first meeting with them went well, so the next thing was to introduce her to my parents. I realized there might be a problem as there are not too many marriages between people of Bangladeshi origin and those of Pakistani origin: the cultures are very distinctive and there are also language barriers. One evening when we were at home Dad and I drove to the Khan chip shop in Ladypool Road. I bought fish and chips and we sat down in the car and I said to him, 'Dad, I want to settle down and get married.'

Let Dad now tell the story of how he reacted and what happened:

I was shocked because never in a million years did I expect him to say I want to get married. We had never spoken to him about arranged marriages, but I was looking for a girl for him for marriage. In the family. I said, 'Oh that is good, Moeen, you want to get married. Settle down.' He said, 'Dad, the only thing is the girl is not from here. She is from London.' I said, 'That's not a problem, Moeen, if you know her.' I am thinking how do you know her? Who introduced her? Moeen said, 'The problem is she is not a Pakistani girl.' I thought there we are, he is going to marry an English girl now. I wasn't against the idea - after all my mother was English. I said, 'Okay, is she an English girl?' He said, 'No. She is from Bangladesh.' I had the fish and chips in my hand and I was thinking how am I going to tell his mother. He said, 'I want to do a Nikah [the Muslim marriage ceremony] now and you can do the rest of it afterwards.' I said, 'Moeen, is everything okay?' He said, 'Yes, Dad. I just want to do a Nikah. I don't want to do the cultural thing.' I said, 'You better get another fish and chips now.' He said, 'Why?' I said, 'You have to tell your mother.'

All the kids were at home. I think he must have told Kadeer or Azba that he was going to talk to me. They were all here waiting for us to come back. My wife didn't know anything about it. That is why he took me out. When we got home we put the fish and chips on the table and I said to my wife, 'Maqsood, I need to talk to you about something. Moeen wants to talk about marriage.' She was open mouthed. 'Marriage?' She was in a bit of shock. She never expected that. I told her the only problem is that she is from Bangladesh. I was looking at her face and she was looking at mine. I could see the redness in her face and was struck by her expression: she did not know whether to be happy or sad. She never expected Moeen to marry a Bangladeshi girl.

I said to my mum, 'Just meet Firuza. If you don't like her, if you don't think she is right, fair enough. But if you think she is not right because she is Bangladeshi then that's not right. She is a Muslim and everything else. She wants to marry somebody like me, a practising Muslim.' Dad's response was prompt. 'No,

Moeen, I have no objections.' Dad did not want to distress me and get me worried, and he agreed to meet Firuza and her family. They went to London. While I played cricket my wife-to-be's family met my mum and dad. This was a new journey for my parents. For a start they had never been to that part of the world. Let Dad take up the story again:

Firuza seemed to be a nice, pretty girl. We were pleased to see she dressed in the style of a practising Muslim woman, covering up with the hijab. We discovered that her parents are from Sylhet in Bangladesh. Then we went to meet her family, only to find that her dad was in Bangladesh and her mum, who was not keen on the marriage, had gone out, leaving just Firuza's siblings to greet us. They were extremely welcoming, but the meeting was not what we had imagined.

The Nikah was in London, and her father remained in Bangladesh but her siblings and aunties came. We had a reception in Birmingham. Her mother is reconciled to Moeen now – I think at first she was overwhelmed by the cultural differences and the language barrier, though both families are Muslim so in that way it was a pretty simple match. Firuza's family did not know anything about him as they did not follow cricket and if they did, would have supported the Bangladeshi team. But while her parents did not approve of him, once they got to know him they liked him. And now they love him. They watch him play all the time.

For the ceremony in Birmingham I was sure how it should be held. I wanted a really old-school occasion, with nothing ostentatious, no fancy cars. I wanted the wedding to represent the fact that Firuza and I are simple, modest people. We had a segregated reception with the women in one hall, the men in another. There was no music, no dancing but a big feast instead – we wanted to have great food, a great laugh and be able to properly talk to our guests. I invited a lot of close friends, many of them from the cricket world including Ben Langley, now the physiotherapist for the England team, and, of course, the wider family of uncles, aunts and cousins. There wasn't – like in many Asian weddings – a stage or anything like that. This was an occasion to enjoy our marriage without putting on a gaudy show. That for me would have been false, artificial and contrary to how my wife and I wanted to lead our life.

CHAPTER 6

THE WORCESTER MAN

had problems when I started at Worcester but they were not man-made. They were made by nature. Floods and the New Road ground are old acquaintances. But, historically, the River Severn bursts its banks in winter and then in the summer the water recedes, (sometimes) the sun comes out and the wicket rolls out perfectly for cricket. In my first season for the county, in 2007, the River Severn burst its banks twenty-four hours before the Twenty20 Cup programme was going to start. On 13 June, Vikram Solanki, the captain, led the team off with rain having brought the Friends Provident 50-over match against Scotland to an end. We all thought this was a brief interruption. We did not play again at New Road for the rest of the season. We became cricket's great nomads in 2007, travelling to Kidderminster, Warwickshire, Derbyshire and even as far as Somerset. We were also scheduled to play at Himley in Staffordshire although, as if the rain was determined to follow us, that match was rained off.

Yet New Road turning into a water park showed the spirit of the side I had joined. One of the most famous stories of the summer was of Steve 'Bumpy' Rhodes swimming across flooded

New Road trying to rescue his laptop. Of Bumpy, the coach, I cannot speak highly enough. Let us just say as a swimmer he is not Michael Phelps – the laptop floated away. It summed up a sense of adventure that was infectious. The moment I walked into the Worcester dressing room I became aware of a very different world to the one in Edgbaston, both welcoming and very understanding of my needs. People were always nice and ready to help. There I was, a kid of twenty in a dressing room full of established players, some like Graeme Hick who had been a star for England, and several senior players who had made their debut long before I was born. Now through Walee's influence my life had changed. I prayed five times a day. But I did not have a spot in the changing room, nor as the rookie could I expect one. But whenever I wanted to pray Hicky, Vik, Gareth Batty and others would readily give up their spots in the dressing room. When Sachin Tendulkar became the first non-white player to play for Yorkshire, Geoffrey Boycott showing him round the Yorkshire dressing room told him to claim a place as there were cricketers there who always wanted their favourite spot. Cricketers cling to their dressing-room spots like leeches. At Worcester, even the most senior players who had sat at the same place in the dressing room for years, understood the needs of the young newcomer. It made me feel very at home.

There was also a family connection, with my cousin Kabir leading the attack and having a great season, taking 56 first-class wickets. In the end the strain proved too much for Kabir and he got injured towards the end of the season. We played together in my first match for the county against Loughborough University at the end of April, long before the floods. I was mostly a bystander, but a proud and happy one, while Kabir destroyed the students, five wickets in the first innings for just 16, six wickets for 39 in the second as we cantered to a ten-wicket victory.

I did not play in a championship match until September but it was still memorable for me because in successive matches in the space of two weeks I batted against two bowlers who were legends to me and who I had always wanted to face: Shane Warne and Mushtaq Ahmed. I got my chance against Warne at Kidderminster when he captained Hampshire. In the first innings, batting number three, I was out long before he came on but in the second innings, as we tried to make an impossible 532 to win, I did face him. I had seen off the Hampshire seamers and then Warne came on to bowl. I had read a lot about Warne sledging but he didn't say anything to me. I watched in awe as the bowler I had seen so often on television now stood at the other end, set the field and then measured out his run-up. The only thought in my head as I faced the first ball was I must hit Warne for a couple of fours. I thought if I do that then whatever else happens I shall always be able to say the first time I faced Shane Warne I hit him for a four. And as he ran in to bowl I was confident I could do that. I knew he was at the end of his career, this was his last season, and his shoulder was giving him trouble. He bowled mostly leg-spinners, a few sliders, he was spinning the ball, but I picked the turn and did hit him for some boundaries. As I hit the first four I looked at him thinking he might say something but he didn't. He did eventually get me out but by then I had scored 77, the highest score in our second innings. It was not enough to avoid defeat with Warne taking five wickets.

A week later I played against Mushtaq Ahmed at Hove. This was an entirely different experience. Mushi was a more classical leg-spinner. More leg breaks, googlies, sliders. Mushtaq was one of my heroes, a Pakistani legend, and he was having another brilliant season for Sussex. Before the match I was wondering if I might face Saqlain Mushtaq as well. Mushi and he had played together. Amazingly I had met Saqlain on the M40 earlier in the season. There was a huge pile-up and everyone started getting out of their cars. As I did so I saw him. He was two cars behind me and I introduced myself and we had a nice chat. I was struck by how friendly he was to someone he had never met and did not know. I did play against him that season in a one-day match but to face Mushi at one end and Saqlain at the other would have been great fun.

As with Warne, I did not face Mushi in the first innings, batting number three and getting out to the seamers for 5. But in the second innings, as we tried to avoid an innings defeat, I did face Mushi. He had taken six wickets in our first innings but the thoughts in my head as Mushi ran in to bowl were the same that I had had when Warny had run in. I must hit my hero for a four. I was very confident in my game and I was playing on instinct. I not only hit Mushi for a four but hit him for a six as well. Like Warne he said nothing, he just got ready to bowl the next ball. This was a great lesson for me. Great players let the ball or the bat do their talking for them. It is only lesser players who use verbals to make up for their playing deficiencies. Mushi did eventually bowl me for 85, and with Mushi taking seven of our last eight wickets, thirteen in the match, our defeat was inevitable. But while I could do nothing about that I had some consolation in that I had made the highest score against the best bowler in the country, whose guile and skill had made Sussex champions. Defeating us gave Sussex their third championship in five seasons and Mushi had been the leading wicket-taker in all three titles. And to think that during that season he was recovering from a World Cup which had seen the sudden death of Bob Woolmer, the Pakistani coach. Never having lived in London, I don't know about waiting for London buses and then finding three of them turning up one after the other. But this was certainly true for Sussex. Sussex had not won the championship for 164 years, and now with an attack led by Mushi they could not stop winning. The only problem for Mushi and the Sussex boys was that having bowled us out half an hour before lunch they had to postpone their celebrations till six as they waited to hear whether Lancashire had beaten Surrey. They had not. While Sussex celebrated we were relegated to Division Two.

But if this was a disappointment in my first season, there was a consolation. The week before we went to Hove we had won our first title in thirteen years, the NatWest Pro-40 League, despite the fact that because of the floods we played home matches at Edgbaston, Derby and Taunton. Nothing that summer gave me more pleasure on the cricket field than the innings I played against Northamptonshire at Kidderminster on 9 September. *Wisden* called it the innings of the season. Batting first on winning the toss, I opened and decided that I would hit every ball I faced. There would be no prodding around to see what the bowling or the wicket was like. I got to my hundred, my first century in senior cricket, from 46 balls with six sixes and fourteen fours. When I got out to the 49th ball I faced, my opening partner Steve Davies, who had captained me when I first played for the England Under-19s, had contributed 31 to the 136-run opening stand. We won by 151 runs and my century was the seventh fastest in what are called List A matches. Had I scored it a ball earlier, I would have equalled the 45-ball hundred Brian Lara had made against Bangladesh, seven years earlier.

But I learnt all that much later. There was a match to be won and also the match four days later at Bristol, a day-night game. This was special for me as I faced Kadeer, playing for Gloucestershire, in a competitive match for the first time. Kadeer made his runs fluently, as he always does, but only 31 and we were set 271 to chase. I opened again and this time Davo and I on a good batting wicket put on 151 in 16 overs, 72 of them mine. We did get worried when the Bristol lights failed. But they were back in fifteen minutes and soon after Hick lost his off-stump. I know players say they do not look at sporting history but Gloucestershire at Bristol has always been our bogey side and there were some twitchy moments in the dressing room. But in the end we held our nerve and ended up winners by six wickets with eleven balls to spare. To win something in my first season for Worcester was sweet indeed.

To complete the trio of great spinners I played against there was also Murali, who I faced in a one-day game at Taunton against Lancashire, with the wicket providing a lot of turn. But that day I actually felt I picked him okay and I didn't feel like it was that much of a problem. I hit him for a six. He was of course a brilliant bowler and I was playing him when he was coming towards the end of his career. With all these three great spinners my first thought on playing them was I must hit them. I never felt overwhelmed or daunted by the prospect of facing up to them.

What was also good about the season was the way Walee was now part of my cricket. While he and I spent most of our time talking about Islam, given his love for the game we also discussed cricket. He was an all-rounder and joked that he saw himself as a sort of right-handed version of Garry Sobers. Once the Worcester deal was done I had told him I was leaving Warwickshire for Worcester. He was delighted for me and told me that with his children living in Cheltenham he would come to see me play. He has kept his word, becoming a regular visitor to New Road, and even now never misses a home match if I am playing. He just phones me and says, 'Mo, leave me a ticket, I'm going to pop in and watch the game for a few hours.'

Right from the beginning when Walee came to watch me at Worcester he would play a game with me. He wouldn't let me know he was there. He would hide behind the big tree which you see as you enter the ground. He would peep out from round the tree to look at the cricket and if he felt I was looking in that direction he would dart back behind the tree. He didn't want to put me off my game. Once I was playing a T20 match. I opened. The first ball was a nice half volley and I hit it. Walee, who was watching from behind the tree, heard the crack of the bat on the ball and thought I had hit a four. What he did not know was it had gone straight to the fielder at cover, who held the catch. When he saw me walking back he realized what had happened and felt that I would be devastated. We were both fasting and the plan was we would have a nice evening meal after we broke our fast. When we got in the car we broke our fast with chewing gum and he started commiserating with me. 'Bro man, you got out early.' I said, 'I creamed it, boy, it felt beautiful off the bat.' He said, 'Bro, when you were caught I thought bloody hell he will be disappointed. He will need cheering up. But you are so cheerful. This shows you have got the right attitude to batting. If a ball is to be hit you hit it no matter if it is the first ball of the match. Do not lose it.'

Walee was there at New Road when I played against Shane Warne. Walee now comes to see me play in Tests and one-dayers travelling round the country. Whenever I score runs and see Walee in the crowd I always raise my bat in his direction. It's almost like I feel he is praying for me when I am playing. I soon found he had a very sharp cricket brain.

He loves the Worcester ground – who wouldn't with its beautiful setting – and during one match after I had got out for a low score we were walking round the ground. As with any county match there were not many people around and as we walked we talked. Walee readily confessed that when we met that day at Edgbaston he didn't know me from Adam and decided to look up my stats and found my innings of 195 which he initially thought must have been a typo. Surely, he told me, 'I thought they got the decimal place wrong and it was really 19. I looked at your stats and you're getting to 35 but you're not going on. When you get to 30 or 35 you should get to a half century and you should go on and build from that. What's going on? How come you're not getting there? What are you thinking? What are you doing? What's happening?' He felt that I lacked confidence and that I had been held back by Warwickshire. I had now come to a new county and I should blossom.

Listening to him, I thought he should be a coach and when I said that to him he asked me why. I replied, 'Because you really made me think about my game.' A week later he had enrolled on a coaching course. He got his level one and level two badges. And as it happened, having listened to Walee, I began to think more about when I got to 30 or 35 and started working on converting 30 or 35 into 50 and then getting tons.

What really touched me was when Walee told his workmates about me and that not only was I a Muslim, but well-mannered and that I was going to play for England. When they asked him how he knew his reply was 'He's got the right attitude and he's a prolific run scorer from when he was young. He's going to get there'.

England was my goal but I could see from the lack of opportunities Kabir had been given it was never going to be easy to persuade the selectors to look at me. It was so exciting when he was selected for the England Test team in 2003. I was in school and someone told me he'd got a wicket in his first over and I remember thinking, wow, he's got an England Test wicket! It was a really big deal to see him play against South Africa at Headingley. Watching Kabir play for England on television was the first time my grandfather appreciated and accepted why my dad and Chacha Shabir had sacrificed so much for so many years.

Kabir ended up taking five wickets on debut but was never picked for the Test team again, even though he had another very good season in 2008, when he was the first bowler in the country to reach 50 championship wickets and four times took five wickets in an innings. But England, who had last selected him in 2006 for the ODI team, clearly didn't want to look again, which I think deep down must have been quite hurtful. This made it clear to me that I must grab whatever chances I got for Worcester but expect nothing. Whenever an opportunity came I tried to make the most of it and during the 2008 season the innings that pleased me most was in the Friends Provident trophy early in the summer at New Road. Two weeks earlier we had played our first match at New Road since June 2007 and the cathedral bells had rung for an hour to celebrate our return. On that Sunday, after Vik and Davo had set up our victory against Hampshire, I decided that, batting at number three, I would not hang about and hit three sixes in an unbeaten 42 not out as we walloped Hampshire by nine wickets.

I was well aware I had joined a county going through change and trying to renew itself. In 2008 Hicky, his eyes all moist, retired at the age of forty-two, and in 2009 several others left including Vik, Gareth Batty and Davo. And poor Kabir who had injury problems also left. There was much media talk of the problems in the county but I did not see it that way. Bumpy had decided that the county had to get young players, and one of his recruits for the season was seventeen-year-old Ben Cox, who took time off from school in our late-September match at Taunton and showed his potential by putting on 124 runs for the seventh wicket.

What that season showed was, even when Worcestershire has problems, the county does not create a drama out of a crisis. There are no major scenes. If things have to be sorted out they are done discreetly behind closed doors. and dealt with on an individual basis. What we don't have is a big team meeting and a lot of dirty linen washed in front of everybody. That has always been the culture of the club ever since I got there and this was set by Vik, the first Worcester captain I played under. From the beginning I felt that this cricket club was like a large family.

The media did not always see it that way and *Wisden* was dismissive of my performances in the 2009 season: 'Moeen Ali,' they wrote, 'failed to make progress.' I don't know what progress they were looking for. I was a regular top-order batsman and often batted when we were struggling to avoid defeat. We were still in the last week of April when I travelled to Leeds and with Vik put on the first stand of over 300 Worcester had ever had for any wicket against Yorkshire. Vik enjoyed a bit of luck, he was dropped twice in scoring 206, and I made 153. I had gone to Headingley having been told that the wicket helped swing and seam. In fact the only thing that moved on a slow pitch was the crane behind the sightscreen at the Kirkstall Lane End where Yorkshire were constructing a new pavilion and media centre.

Vik and I made sure we drew the match and I felt I had nearly contributed to another draw against Sussex in early June when, 322 behind, Daryl Mitchell and I came together at 73 for 3 and put on 208 in 62 overs, Mitch just missing out on a century while I went on to make 124. But then I gloved a leg-side loosener by James Kirtley and the Indian leg-spinner Piyush Chawla, whom I had played against in Under-19 cricket and who was making his county debut, went on to seal victory for Sussex. And at Taunton at the end of the season there was one memory to treasure. I had my hero Trescothick stumped.

The innings I really enjoyed was early in April when in the Friends Provident trophy at Southampton we made 320 for 8 in 50 overs and I made 125, my highest one-day score, in 109 balls with nine fours and three sixes. I didn't get my century with a six – but I got to 99 with one. It was a close-run thing. On 93 I lofted the ball and Billy Taylor held the catch on the boundary but toppled over the ropes.

Despite how the media saw the season, what Bumpy was doing was building up young players and it all came good in 2010. The media dubbed us the 'Yo-Yoing Young Turks'. On 12 August after a crushing defeat at Colwyn Bay we were 37 points adrift of leaders Glamorgan, and 36 behind Sussex. Promotion back to Division One seemed an impossible dream. But we won all three of our remaining matches and we returned to Division One. The chairman Martyn Price praised Mitch, Alexei Kervezee and me and now it was the turn of the media to yo-yo. *Wisden* said, 'Moeen's talent had never been in question, but he was more disciplined and possessed a stomach for a battle – especially when plundering 337 runs in a week in late April.' I headed the batting averages, with 1,260 runs at an average of 48.46, and my 17 wickets also had one five-wicket haul.

That week in April was indeed special, beginning with the second day of the match against Surrey at Whitgift School in Croydon. Surrey, on winning the toss, had made 493 with football's 'law of the ex' operating where a former player performs very well against his old team. 'Davo' Davies, who had defected to Surrey, scored a hundred as Surrey accumulated their imposing total. I came in to bat with our score 0 for 2 but by the end of the day was 122 not out and with Vik had put on 223 for the third wicket, a Worcester record against Surrey. In the second innings another ex, Gareth Batty, might have spun us to defeat but fortunately I was dropped on 16 and made 72 not out to get a draw. It was also good in that I was used as a main spinner in both innings and ended up with four wickets, two of them batsmen I had often bowled to in the Worcester nets: Davo in the first innings after he had got 137, and in the second their captain Rory Hamilton-Brown.

Three days later back in Worcester I came in to bat with the score 10 for 2. The Glamorgan fast bowler David Harrison was causing mayhem on a wicket where he was getting steep bounce bowling just short of a length. I decided the only way was to take the attack to him, hitting 85 not out in 135 balls with thirteen fours. But others found Harrison impossible, and he took seven wickets. Only one other batsman made double figures (15), and we were bowled out for 134, with Harrison taking a seven-wicket haul. In the second innings the damage was done by his opening partner James Harris and although I again top scored, with 58, it was never going to be enough.

But individual feats in a losing effort never mean as much as when you help your team win and this was illustrated when we went to Leicester. They had won both their opening matches and when we batted on winning the toss it seemed Matthew Hoggard had rediscovered his old England form. Once again I came in needing to steady the ship after we had lost cheap early wickets, with the score 15 for 2. *Wisden* would later describe my innings, the highest in our total, as a 'high-class 80, which included 18 off a [Claude] Henderson over and was harsh on anything loose', and launched Worcestershire towards a respectable first innings score. That, combined with good bowling from our seamers and good solid second innings batting where I made 42, was enough to give us victory.

Now I was going into bat confident I could make runs and when at the end of May Gloucester came to New Road I scored my second century of the summer, 106, scoring at six an over, but rain meant our first innings advantage was not enough to win.

I missed a century against Gloucestershire in early August at the Cheltenham festival but played a part in our unexpected win. Having scored their season's highest score, 480, Gloucestershire decided not to enforce the follow-on as the captain for that game, Alex Gidman, thought his bowlers were tired and set us 399 to win. Mitch Mitchell, who had scored a century in the first innings – I had helped him with 59 – made another, I got 94 and we won by six wickets. There is nothing quite as satisfying as proving the opposing captain wrong.

But although we lost the next match against Glamorgan and seemed doomed to stay in Division Two we won three of the following four games, defeating Surrey and Sussex at home and Middlesex at Lord's. I shall always remember that Lord's win for it showed I was not just a batsman who occasionally turned his arm. I could be considered an all-rounder. With the bat I was top scorer in both innings, with 66 and 81. The home team certainly thought there would be nothing in the wicket for spin for they dropped Shaun Udal and played an extra batsman. Shakib Al Hasan, our overseas signing from Bangladesh whom I had played against in the Under-19 World Cup, was our main spinner, but with Middlesex going well I was brought on, got their centurion Owais Shah out and took four more wickets to finish with a five-fer for the first time in my first-class career. Shakib came into his own in the second innings, taking seven wickets, and we bowled out the hosts for just 66, winning easily.

The season had a wonderful finish as on the last day at New Road in a rain-affected match, Sussex, who were already promoted, set us a target of 300 in 70 overs. The pitch was two-paced, the highest score had been 264 but we knew we had nothing to lose. If Glamorgan, also contesting the second promotion spot, won, we could do nothing. I came in with the score 44 for 2, with fellow left-hander James Cameron, who had never opened before, at the other end. We decided we had to go for it and in 35.4 overs put on 215, James scoring his maiden century. By the end I felt so comfortable that after I got to 115 I decided to have a swish and got out but by then we could not lose. Our victory by six wickets came with 15 overs to spare. The only problem was Glamorgan were still playing and we had to wait an hour before we heard they had not won and we were up.

The T20 tournament did not bring us any joy although I had reason to look back with satisfaction when we played a floodlit match at Derby. In such matches the Man of the Match does not often play for the losing side but the adjudicators decided that I was that player despite the fact that Derbyshire won by six wickets. In our 127 for 7 in 20 overs, I made 67 and then took 2 for 14 in 4 overs of what the media called 'tidy off-spin'.

And while we lost to Nottinghamshire easily, I faced Broady for the first time and was quite pleased with my 67. I was Man of the Match again when we beat Leicester, but that was for my bowling figures of 3 for 19 as we restricted Leicestershire to 142 for 8 and won by three wickets.

Experts say Sunday 40-overs cricket makes no sense as there is no international competition. But it is always great fun and for me the best match was in late August at New Road when against Glamorgan I made 121 in our score of 296 for 5. Initially I struggled to find the boundary, taking 22 balls to hit my first, but then took 19 balls to get to my 50 and would have scored quicker had the match been played six weeks later. Twice Tom Maynard fielding at long-on backed beyond the ropes and threw the ball back into the field when airborne. The rule change that was introduced shortly thereafter would have seen them count as sixes.

But I had reason enough to see the season as a success. We were not a rich county – as Bumpy said we were not conveyed in grand coaches, we often shared rooms on our travels – but we had some decent cricketers. Money has never meant anything to me playing cricket. I had come to Worcester because I wanted to be sure I would get a chance to play in the first team. Bumpy had lived up to the promise he had made to Dad. He had provided me with opportunities. I started off at Worcester batting at six and then I got pushed up the order to five, four and then eventually number three, which is where I have been batting for the last few years and which I think is my ideal position. In the one-dayers I was opening. Bumpy Rhodes was somebody who had always helped me with my game right from the start and pushed me in training. I knew I could do even better. When Worcester offered me a three-year contract I readily signed.

I was happy within myself. I had a wonderful wife who was incredibly supportive of my career, attending as many matches as she could and being very understanding about the need for constant travel, and on the cricket field there were no problems created by my faith. Early on at Worcester I had heard a shout from a spectator saying 'shave it off', a reference to my beard. And a Worcester scout had suggested that as well. But all that was history. The county, the players, the coaching staff and the supporters accepted me as I was, a Muslim, but also as one of them and the wider society and multicultural world to which we in Britain are so proud to belong.

I was still a Sparkhill boy. Nothing would change that and after a day's play nothing gave me greater pleasure than to drive back to my roots. But I was now a Worcester man.

CHAPTER 7

WILL ENGLAND EVER CALL?

t is not difficult to mark moments when important events happen in your life. Moments you treasure. One such cricketing moment for me was at Manchester on the evening of 11 April 2013. We were due to play a county championship match against Lancashire at Old Trafford the next day. But the setting was not Old Trafford but a snooker table in the city centre.

Not long after we had gathered at our Manchester hotel Bumpy came up to me and said, 'Let's go and play some snooker.' I knew that was his way of relaxing and it is mine as well. Whenever we go to Manchester we always play snooker. There is a snooker bar opposite the hotel where we stay in the city centre. I like snooker. I am no Steve Davis, but I play a lot. I like all sports, give me a racket, table tennis, badminton or football and I want to play. After we had played, Bumpy sat me down and said, 'I want to sign a new deal.' I said, 'Look, I'll sign a five-year deal'. I was a month short of my 26th birthday and about to become a father. It was now six years since I had first turned out for Worcestershire, five since I made my Worcester debut but England had not come calling. I had given up any hopes of ever getting an England cap. I thought, you know what; it's not going to happen so I'm just going to be the best county player I can be. The Worcester deal Bumpy was offering was to secure my future with the county that had done so much for me. It made perfect sense.

The media were surprised that an aspiring England player, as they described me, had committed himself for so long to a Division Two club. They were keen to find out why as I made it clear I could have earned more money at another club. The facilities could be better but Worcester had been good to me. I enjoyed being one of the main men in the team. Now that Vik Solanki had left for Surrey I had added responsibilities and I was happy to take them on. I liked the Worcester people. Money was not everything although Bumpy had offered me a good deal. That evening after the snooker we also discussed cricket and my batting technique.

Over the years Bumpy had tried to make my technique better. I had gone through a lot of changes in my batting style. My problem was I kept being lbw in county cricket. It was not a question of playing in front of my pads, the reason many batsmen get lbw. My problem was slower swing bowlers in county cricket. When playing them my head would fall over to the off-side and my right leg would go across and the natural consequence was I would be lbw. In order to correct that I decided I would have a stance like Shivnarine Chanderpaul, so that, I thought, whatever happens I'm not going to get lbw. We could not be two more different batsmen. Chanderpaul is a very defensive batsman but very difficult to get out, very steady and I wanted some of his consistency. Adopting Chanderpaul's stance, I managed then to work on my balance and technique. I knew eventually I'd have to come back to my own style, but my hope was that by being Chanderpaul I would return with a tighter technique. Bumpy was fine with what I was doing. He's been around for so long he knew I was going through a transition as a batter and I'm always wanting to learn how to improve.

I began the 2013 season aware that I had my moments in 2011 and 2012 but not the consistency I wanted. Moeen Ali, said *Wisden* of the 2011 season, 'showed only flashes of his power and potential' and I was inclined to agree. So, just as May turned to June in 2011, I helped beat Nottinghamshire, the defending champions, in our first top-flight win for 27 matches, going back to 2007, and our first at New Road in seven years. In reply to Nottinghamshire's 223, my 84 ensured we made 243, a small but useful lead. Then set 255 to win, I came in to bat when the score was 117 for 2, our first wicket going on 0; I was 35 not out when we won by six wickets.

There were other moments to savour, although in losing causes. A month before the Nottinghamshire victory I made 92 against Warwickshire, giving us a first innings lead of 174 but good batting by the visitors and a dreadful second-innings display meant defeat by 88 runs. I probably had my best championship innings against Somerset, also at New Road at the end of July, when I made a career-best 158, getting my sweep in order against the Indian left-arm spinner Murali Kartik. At the end of the first day we were 367 for 3 and I was 134 not out. But the next day I added only 24 and we lost seven wickets for 121. This showed that even a first-innings score of 488 is no insurance against defeat. My hero, Trescothick, rubbed home the point of what you do when you have got in and are on top of the bowling. You don't let them escape. One century is not enough. As Walee kept telling me, when you have done all the hard work make sure you make it count and turn it into a really big score. Trescothick made 203. We batted dreadfully in the second innings, scraping together only 95 in 39 overs and lost by an innings and 8 runs.

There were matches where my batting secured victory, such as against Sussex in Horsham in August when with innings' of 71 and 68 we won by 34 runs. This made up for a defeat at the end of July which had stung quite a bit. It came in the Clydesdale Bank 40 and, as was the pattern for one-day matches, I opened chasing Sussex's 399. Horsham, a very pleasant little ground, was packed and I saw no reason why we could not get that. I had a bit of luck, dropped on 2, but made 158 in 92 deliveries, the highest score of the competition and the second best in Worcestershire's 40-over history. The match aggregate of 718 was another record in the format, 436 coming in boundaries. But with the next highest score of just 35 we lost by 80 runs. This match was followed by a home match against the Netherlands and I scored another century, 117, and we lost again by two wickets. By now losing to the Dutchmen was not a total disgrace. This was their fourth county scalp and in 2009 they had beaten England in a T20 World Cup match at Lord's.

In 2011 I had played alongside Saeed Ajmal and he had taught me the doosra, how to grip the ball and the things you need to do with your body. I found the actual technique of bowling the doosra pretty easy. The ICC were later to look into the legality of Ajmal's action and I must admit that in bowling the doosra there is definitely a problem. It's tough to bowl it with a straight arm. You've got to have some sort of bend in the arm. Some people bend it less than others. But I don't spin my doosra as much. It's just different to my off-spinner. I was always careful with it. I must confess when I heard the ICC action against Saeed I was surprised but as long as they feel like they're doing the right thing and they're challenging everybody who they think has a suspect action, then it's fair enough.

I had begun the 2012 season determined to shed this image of being a batsman who bowled. I bowled more than I had ever bowled for Worcester both in the county championship and the one-day matches and was second in the bowling averages for the championship with 33 wickets. I was being seen as the county's major spinner and it was wonderful to go to Old Trafford in mid-July and take six wickets in both innings. My 6 for 67 in the first was a career best, but in the second I bettered that taking 6 for 29 as Lancashire, chasing 269, were bowled out for 65, their lowest total on their home ground since 1963. A win is a win, but a win on the opposition ground where they have prepared a wicket which provided turn was very special.

I was also taking wickets in the one-day matches. We were still in May when I took three wickets in the Clydesdale Bank 40 in consecutive overs against Middlesex, bowling us to a 56-run victory. For the first time my bowling won me a Man of the Match award when we beat Northamptonshire at Northampton in the Friends Life T20, conceding just 14 runs in 4 overs as we defended our score of 142 for 5 to give us a 14-run victory. A week earlier I had also won the Man of the Match award at New Road, but this was for my batting when I scored a competition-best 82 off 44 balls, and we beat Gloucestershire by 47 runs. I also much savoured our victory over Somerset at Taunton when opening the batting I got to 47 in 23 balls and we never lost momentum after that. I wish we could have done better against Yorkshire in the quarter-finals but despite losing the match was memorable for me for a stunning piece of fielding by Joe Root. Fielding on the deep midwicket boundary as the ball from James Cameron came over, Rooty caught it, but the moment took him over the ropes and he tossed the ball to David Miller to make sure of the catch. This has become commonplace now, with Ben Stokes in the Indian Premier League in 2017 taking this to a new level, but in 2012 it was quite a novelty.

I had gone into that Manchester snooker hall pretty confident and ready for the season. I wasn't looking too far ahead. In terms of cricket I was very content within myself. I just wanted to be a good county player. I think that really helped my game that year. I took one day at a time. I worked hard. There were no special ingredients, just be in the present and enjoy myself. My chat with Bumpy had further energized me although rain was the big winner in the opening championship encounter of 2013. However, I made a start with 78, the top scorer in our innings. And on a wicket that aided swing and where lights were used for the first time in a championship match, I bowled 21 overs, taking the wicket of Lancashire's Australian signing, Simon Katich. I knew I had to carry on from there and was determined to do so. Before May was over there were innings that both gave me pleasure and won us matches. My 54 at Canterbury in mid-May meant we did not fritter away the advantage of bowling Kent out for 159 and the lead of 38 became unbeatable when our opening bowler Alan Richardson took 7 for 22. I took the catch for his first wicket with the Kent score on 0. We bowled them out for 63 and by the second evening we had won by 10 wickets.

I had set a target of being consistent and in the matches that followed I regularly made runs and took wickets. It was nice to collect accolades with *Wisden* highlighting my innings at Northampton, 79 and 44 not out in a match we lost by ten wickets: 'Throughout Ali was head and shoulders above his team mates on a spicy wicket, but he could not see off [Trent] Copeland and [David] Willey [the Northants opening bowlers] on his own.'

The first of my four centuries that season came in the third week of May against Gloucestershire, which *Wisden* described as a 'delicious hundred'. My century ensured we made the most of Richardson's superb bowling, taking 12 wickets in the match

– he was to have a sensational last season at the age of thirty-four. But pleasing as the innings was, I did kick myself for I had ended the second day's play 122 not out. The next day I added only one run. It made me more determined to make sure that when I got a century I would make it a big one.

I had to wait a month for that and it was again at New Road. We were put in by Glamorgan, I came in with the score 12 for 1; at the end of the first day's play I was 155 not out. My partner Matthew Pardoe, another left-hander, made 102, and we were 322 for 3. The next day I batted another session and a half, making 250 and when I was seventh out at 498 we declared. At that stage I was the country's highest run-getter on 900, ahead of Rooty, and only the eighth Worcester batsman to reach 250. And then in late August when Lancashire called I made a hundred in each innings, which meant I had done a double of three hundreds and two fifties in my last seven championship innings at New Road. By the time the championship season ended I had scored 1,375 runs at an average of 62.50, which easily put me top of the Worcester batting averages, with the next batsman averaging 39.00. I was also proud of my 22 catches.

What pleased me was these runs in four-day cricket did not mean my one-day performances withered. Under the lights at Northampton at the end of July in the Friends Life T20, I had my best one-day performance, 72 with six fours and four sixes, three in one over, and taking five Northants wickets for 34 runs. And while I did not see myself as more determined to do well when I faced my home county in the day-night match in the Yorkshire Bank 40 in mid-August at Edgbaston, I scored 114 from 85 balls, my seventh one-day century. All in all I ended the season scoring 1,420 first-class runs, the highest tally in the country, and Wisden was complimentary: 'He has always been pleasing on the eye but had now settled on a more compact stance, and resolved to leave everything outside the off-stump before getting to 20.' They also noted that I was rare among England off-spinners in bowling the doosra. According to Wisden, 'For the first time he was in the running for an England spot.'

I had never had a summer like this. I had scored more than 2,000 runs in all forms of the game and had taken 55 wickets. I was voted Professional Cricketers' Association Player of the Year. As I accepted the award, surrounded by my friends and rivals, I thought that perhaps an England selector would finally pick up the phone and say, 'Moeen, you are in the England squad.' That call never came. The call I got was not to play Test cricket but to go to Loughborough to be part of the Performance Squad which, as the England Lions, would tour Australia in the winter and then play in Sri Lanka.

When I told Dad he was absolutely gutted. He had been sure that after the season I'd had I must be in the squad. I told him that I thought my England ambition was now over. But then I added, more to console him, 'You never know about next year.' I was also aware of history, and mindful of Kabir's experience. England had selected a few Asian cricketers and they had all played one or two matches and fizzled out. The invitation to be part of the Performance Squad convinced me that whatever I did England would never call. I knew I was ready to play for England, wanted to play for England but if after the summer I'd had I was not considered good enough then when would I be? However, as I drove to Loughborough I was not too fussed. If I played for England – fine. If not, that was fine also. I would just enjoy my cricket as I had done in the summer of 2013. I was calm in myself, I was content already. For the other wonderful thing that happened in 2013 was that Firuza and I became parents to an incredible little boy, Abu Bakr. I named him Abu Bakr in honour of the great Abu Bakr as-Siddiq, the close friend of the Holy Prophet who became the first follower of Islam and was celebrated for his unshakeable faith. I'm extremely proud to have my son bear such a powerful and meaningful name. I was always told that kids will bring blessings and it's such a true statement. Having a child is an absolute miracle and to this day I can't believe he's my son. I loved Abu Bakr instantly and was determined to raise him with the humility and dedication and joy that my parents had bestowed on me.

And it was really important to me that my grandmother Betty got to hold my son before she died. Late in her life she circled back to the Islamic faith she'd embraced during her years of marriage to my grandfather, and on the first day of Ramadan the year before she died she told me she wanted to revert back to being Muslim. I was elated by this news and although I was travelling at the time, I asked Walee to visit her and give her the Shahada to officially bring her back to Islam. He recorded the ceremony so I could listen to it later – he found it incredibly moving and was in tears. Five months after that she became very ill and started to lose her memory. When I would visit her in hospital, Dad would tell her to touch my face and my beard and she would acknowledge me, even though she couldn't recognize most people by that stage. She was an incredibly wise and kind person and I feel blessed to have had her in my life.

CHAPTER 8

FINALLY!

On the first day of our camp at Loughborough all the Performance Squad were assembled together. The coaching staff had all gathered: Ashley Giles, Dave Parsons, Hugh Morris, Paul Downton. And there must have been five or six selectors present. We were asked to explain (in a twist on *Dragon's Den* they called Lion's Den) why we felt England should invest in us. What we would bring to the national team. We were supposed to write down our thoughts and then make a presentation to the England hierarchy. I decided I wasn't going to write anything. I walked in without any notes. The first question they asked me was, 'Why should we invest in you?'

I looked straight at them and said, 'If you pick me, you pick me. If you don't pick me I am still happy, and I am still content. But if you pick me I will give my hundred per cent every time. I have had one of my best seasons for Worcestershire and I feel I am ready to play for England. If I am picked, then it is fine, and if I'm not, that's also fine. There is more to life than cricket and cricket is not my be-all and end-all.' I took a mere thirty seconds to say it. I was not worried about being so blunt. Then they asked me a few questions about the season just gone, and I went through some of the highlights. Amazingly, the fact that I had laid it out so bluntly went down quite well with everybody there.

The Lions squad was full of players who were all hoping to play for England. The player I immediately bonded with was Chris Jordan of Sussex. He'd had a good season for Sussex and had been much praised in the media for his aggressive fast bowling. He had played for England in the one-day internationals that summer. I soon discovered that he had no airs and that he was a warm, fantastic guy. We got on so well together that every evening as I sat in the balcony of my room in the hotel, which was part of the university complex, he would join me, and we would talk. We told each other, 'Imagine playing for England and making our Test debuts.' Little did we imagine then that in just over six months, on a sunny June Thursday at Lord's, we would be making our Test debut together. On the second day of that Test as we took the field I was fielding at cover and he was at point and I went up to him and I said, 'I can't believe we are playing Test cricket.' It was such a surreal feeling. Those winter evenings at Loughborough, looking out at the splendid sports facilities of the university, Chris and I were full of the dreams that we all have when it seems we will never fulfil our objectives. However, as we left England for Australia I made a mental resolution.

I had gone in with the mindset that I was ready to play for England, but even if it never happened I'd show what I could do. I would train hard, I would give my all. I would have a good time, enjoy myself, because I didn't want to look back and say I hadn't done the best I could. I didn't want to have any regrets. I had been on a Lions tour to India at the age of twenty-one, but I had come back that time thinking I hadn't done my best. This time I wanted to come back from the tour thinking I had really enjoyed it, that it had been a good tour and I'd made good friends.

There was another difference with that Lions tour. In India I was one of the younger players. This time I was one of the senior players and part of a strong side with Mark Wood, Chris Woakes, who had made his Test debut in the last Ashes Test of the summer, the captain, James Taylor, Varun Chopra, Liam Plunkett and me. But there were also a couple of young players around, like Alex Lees, Tymal Mills and Ben Foakes, and I felt I should make them feel valued and not under pressure in any way. I wanted to bring the younger players in and for them to come back feeling they had got on really well and had a good time.

Australia was a spot of training, more fitness work and a couple of games. It was not a great time to be an English cricketer down under and we watched the Australians win the Test series 5-0, only the third 5-0 whitewash in an Ashes series, and as we were flying to Sri Lanka in late January we lost the one-day internationals 4-1. Defeats cause chaos but this tour was exceptional. Jonathan Trott had come back after the first Test for what was described as 'stress-related illness', Graeme Swann quit cricket after the defeat at Perth in the third Test and as we prepared to fly to Sri Lanka Andy Flower quit as coach.

There was much media speculation as to who might take over with some suggesting it could be Mark Robinson, the Sussex coach who was running our Lions side. One of the Lions did make it to the full England team. Chris Jordan was called up for the Twenty20 internationals against Australia. I was delighted for him but, in keeping with the resolution I had made when I left England, I didn't anticipate any such a call-up for me. What I wanted to do was enjoy my cricket in Sri Lanka, a country I knew and whose people I loved.

One of the features of a Lions tour is that you don't receive much press attention, but on this tour it was even less than usual as most of the media were concerned with Kevin Pietersen, who had been dropped after the Test series with much talk that his England career might be over, all the more so as England's new managing director Paul Downton emphasized the need for a fresh 'team ethic and philosophy'. I started well in the first match against the Sri Lanka A Emerging Players, making 53. I soon found that having come as the third, even fourth spinner after Ollie Rayner, Scott Borthwick and Simon Kerrigan, I was bowling as much as them and performing well.

My batting form carried on in the first unofficial Test where, batting number five, I made 70, the highest score in our innings, and bowled a total of 26 overs in the match, taking four wickets. I was particularly pleased with my two wickets for 16 in the first innings where both my victims were top order batsmen. We won by 167 runs. It was just after this that the phone rang. England wanted me. I was to go immediately to the West Indies where

England were playing one-day internationals, trying to recover from the 4-1 drubbing in Australia.

I rang Dad to say I was on my way to the West Indies. He was delighted but I told him, 'Dad, don't get too excited, you're only going to be disappointed when I get dropped. I may not be picked in any case.' Not that I was anxious. I wanted to dampen his spirits as I felt I was not going to be selected and I knew how devastated he had been when I didn't receive an England call after my 2013 season.

With the team having already departed for the Caribbean I flew out on my own, joining them in Antigua. For me this was a new world. I'd never been to the West Indies before. I had played with most of the players but apart from Chris Jordan, I didn't know anybody properly. And they didn't know me. At that time, apart from CJ, nobody called me Brother Mo. Although Joe Root and Eoin Morgan were in the side, Stuart Broad, who was going to take the team to the World Twenty20 which was to start in Bangladesh on 16 March, three days after our tour ended, was captain. Called in at short notice, I went straight into the one-day internationals with no preparation time.

I knew Ashley Giles from Warwickshire and had played the odd net session with him. But at Warwickshire he would speak to everybody apart from me. He was the county's spin bowler and never once spoke to me about bowling spin. For whatever reason, we never really got on. He said nothing to me when I arrived at Antigua and the night before the first one-day international I had no idea I was playing. I knew there were a couple of injuries. Alex Hales had done his hamstring and Luke Wright was also injured. I didn't know who was likely to play in their places. I went off with Chris Jordan, Ravi Bopara and some of the lads to a restaurant called Miracles, down the road from the hotel. We had eaten there almost every night, the staff looked after us and I had developed a liking for Caribbean food, jerk chicken and all that kind of stuff. Then suddenly my phone rang. It was Ashley Giles. I thought: why is he phoning me? He's never phoned me. He was very brief: 'I'll just prepare you, you're going to open the batting tomorrow.' And then he put the phone down. Clive Lloyd tells the story that when he made his Test debut for the West Indies in 1966 he got half an hour's notice. He was at the nets in Mumbai on the morning of the first Test when Garry Sobers, the captain, came up to him and told him he was playing. So, I suppose I should be grateful that I got a whole night to think about making my England debut. The boys were delighted for me and felt that Miracles had lived up to its name.

I was, obviously, excited to be making my debut at the Sir Vivian Richards ground, named after Dad's all-time hero. The day before the match Sir Vivian had unveiled a bronze statue of himself in the forecourt of the stadium. But half an hour before the match during the warm-up there was a problem. Ben Stokes and I were throwing balls at each other. We had mittens on – we were trying to warm up our shoulders – and I started messing around with him and I put one just on the floor. Stokesy, who has got such power – he doesn't know his own power half the time – decided he would mess around as well and he hit me straight in my left thumb. I knew I'd done something to it. I spoke to the physio, Craig de Weymarn. I said, 'Look, I know I've fractured my thumb. Yeah. Definitely fractured, because I've done it before.' The physio then taped it up.

We won the toss and put them in. As a right-handed bowler my injured thumb didn't affect me and I bowled 6 overs, getting one of the Bravo brothers, Darren, lbw for 2 which reduced the West Indies to 45 for 4. But our bowling at the death was not good and the West Indies scored 100 from the last seven overs, getting to 269 with Dwayne making 87 not out. During the innings break Curtly Ambrose, Richie Richardson and Andy Roberts, all great Antiguans, received their knighthoods, which made me aware of how honoured I was to make my international debut in such a setting in front of such cricketing legends.

Michael Lumb, who was also making his debut, had come in for Alex Hales and opened with me. Michael and I talked as we walked out, two debutants together. Michael was going to take the first ball. I couldn't feel my left hand and I knew there were certain shots I couldn't really play. But with my adrenalin rushing I wasn't nervous at all. Not even when I faced my first ball in international cricket, bowled by Ravi Rampaul. All I wanted was to make sure I got my first run. As Rampaul came in to bowl I decided I would just block. It was not a deliberate shot. But it ran down to third man off the edge giving me a single. The conditions were certainly something I was not used to. The

Caribbean light is very different to anything I had faced, it has a haze. The wind factor was huge. But all that didn't bother me. I knew I had to adjust and I did so. What was a problem was the wicket was slow and the ball did not come on to the bat, despite this being the ground of Roberts and Ambrose, and it was difficult to score. I managed to get 44 and Michael and I put on 96 for the first wicket. That should have been a platform to get to the West Indian score. But whereas they had prospered at the end of their innings, we crumbled, surrendering four wickets for 31 runs in 6 overs to lose the game by 15 runs.

It was after my innings that Giles came up to me and he said, 'It's like you've been playing international cricket for a while. You were so very calm at the crease.' He had never ever said anything to me and to hear such praise was both unexpected and very nice. However, what I couldn't tell him was that I had fractured my thumb. I had finally got my chance to play for England and, fractured thumb or not, I wasn't going to give anyone a chance to drop me. So, for every game I taped it up. The physio, of course, knew but he clearly kept it from Giles.

All the three internationals were in Antigua and in the second, despite my fractured thumb, I managed to take a return catch to dismiss Kieran Powell for 16. And this time we did not squander our advantage and having bowled the West Indies for 159, with Rooty dismissing their opener and the number three, we won. For the final match Antigua produced a wicket very different to the previous two. This was an abrasive pitch where the ball could suddenly bounce. Rampaul certainly made the ball rear and I had to make sure I protected my left hand. For me the innings was memorable as it was the first time I had a stand with Rooty. I got 55 and put on 78 for the third wicket. Rooty made a brilliant 107, his first one-day international century, despite the fact that the third ball he faced Rampaul hit him on the right thumb and the bone broke into eight pieces. His batting and that of Jos Buttler meant we made our highest ever total in the Caribbean, 303. Rooty for good measure opened the bowling and got a wicket in his first over. I got Darren Bravo out again and we won by 25 runs and the series 2-1.

The West Indies reversed the result in the three T20 matches but for both sides this was more of a warm-up for the World Cup in Bangladesh. I was now an England player and going back to a country I knew, had visited often, and where I had played in the Bangladesh Premier League a year earlier and much enjoyed the experience. We flew straight from Barbados to Dhaka. The spirits were good, and we had no way of knowing how bad things would be.

Maybe things might have turned out differently had forked lighting and Duckworth Lewis not intervened in our very first match against New Zealand at Chittagong. Brendon McCullum had put us in and we lost Hales to the third ball of the match. From my berth at number three I found this was a wicket where I could pull to my heart's content and Lumb and I put on 72 in 6 overs. I made 36, the highest score in our innings of 172 for 6. It was certainly competitive but despite the fact that lightning soon lit up the dark Chittagong night, the umpires did not call off play. They allowed New Zealand to bat for 5 overs. This meant it was a match. McCullum shrewdly ensured that before heavy rain brought the match to a close New Zealand were ahead on the Duckworth Lewis calculations and we lost. Broady, who can get very emotional, was furious and his outburst against the umpires meant he was fined 15 per cent of his match fee. But if this was bad luck, the rest of our cricket in the tournament was terrible. There is no disguising that we were bad. We just didn't know how to play T20s. The only glimmer was our victory over Sri Lanka, the eventual champions, who we beat quite handily by six wickets, but given we lost to South Africa and even the Netherlands it was never going to be enough.

When I came back from the disastrous World Twenty20 tournament I didn't see myself as an England player. I had played for England, but did that mean I would be picked again? No. I knew there were quite a few players who had played a couple of games, maybe three or four, and then just vanished from the England scene. I did feel that I had done enough to be around the set-up and they probably liked the look of me. Then after the Twenty20 debacle Ashley Giles got the sack, his dreams of becoming England coach in ruins, Peter Moores took over and that was when the tide turned for me.

Now the Test call-up I had been waiting for finally came.

CHAPTER 9

THE BEARD RETURNS TO LORD'S

On the morning of 12 June 2014 I arrived at Lord's for my Test debut, carrying my son and with my beard properly trimmed. For me both were statements. My son was showing what my family had always meant to me. Firuza was at Lord's. So were Mum and Dad. My beard, as I have always said, was part of my Muslim identity. The beard was now well known on the county circuit and caused no comment. But I was aware that this was the first time the wider English cricketing world would be exposed to it.

As I went through the Grace Gates I looked at the imposing statue of W. G. Grace who had the most famous beard in the history of the game. Just over a month after my Test debut the *Daily Mail* wrote an article comparing Grace's beard with mine, noting that in Victorian times doctors often suggested it was good to grow beards as it was useful for catching impurities in the air. I had heard stories about Grace's beard including the one about batting in a game against Australia in 1896, when a ball bowled at W.G. went straight through his beard. I doubted whether I would have any such experience against the Sri Lankans.

It was just a month earlier that I had received a phone call from James Whittaker telling me that I was going to play in the first Test against Sri Lanka. I had no worries that it was a fake call. I arrived in London three days before the match. We stayed at the Langham, opposite the BBC and my family, my mum, everybody was there.

I woke up on the morning of the Test feeling very relaxed. I knew Bumpy Rhodes and Daryl Mitchell, the Worcester captain, were also going to be at Lord's. As I drew back the curtains I could see the sun was shining and I thought about what lay ahead. I had put in the hours, I had worked hard in the Lord's nets at the Nursery End for a couple of days before the match and I felt ready. Although I was in the side for my batting, as the only spinner I knew I would get a fair amount of bowling.

Lord's as ever was a picture and I was one of three debutants, Chris Jordan and Sam Robson being the others. Just before the start we had a huddle outside the pavilion and then Mike Gatting gave me my England cap. He made a really good speech about what it means to play for England. Alastair Cook put us at ease. He told me, 'Just enjoy it, do what you do for Worcester.' The other guys also tried to keep me relaxed. While I was making my debut Liam Plunkett was making a comeback, playing his first Test after seven years. How cricketing fortunes can swing.

On a greenish Lord's wicket, probably fearing our pace attack, Sri Lanka put us in and as I was number six in the order I was able to watch a bit of the play. If I'm batting next I lie down and shut my eyes for a little bit and then get back up. I knew there would be eyes on me, a lot of people that had never seen me play before, especially at Lord's. With the special atmosphere of that place I wasn't sure what to expect, but as Ian Bell got out and I walked out of the dressing room, down the stairs, then turned right to go through the Long Room as my name was called, I received a massive cheer. I thought, everybody knows me, I'm making my England debut, and that really settled me down. I heard the huge roar from the Lord's crowd as I walked down the steps to the pitch. That support gave me great comfort. And I felt very reassured knowing my family were sitting on the right side of the pavilion at the Tavern End.

Naturally I sensed a little bit of pressure, but I also knew that I was ready for this. My attitude was, I'm here to play for England. I'm here to show that I can play for England. As I walked out to the middle I concentrated and decided to treat my debut as just another game. What I needed to do was switch on by the time I got to the wicket.

We were 120 for 4 and in some trouble. My first few balls I left and then Shaminda Eranga ran in and bowled one straight and I clipped it. I didn't know where the ball went. It was like a blur for a second and then I just ran and the ball raced away for four. And after that I was fine. I didn't think I was going to get a nought, once I'd clipped it I knew I'd nailed it. I knew I'd middled it. Dad couldn't watch as I hit my first four in Test cricket. He had turned his face away as Eranga bowled and only turned back to see the play when he heard the cheers of the crowd. The media the next day noted that I was watchful outside the off-stump but played with a flourish on the leg-side and just missed my half-century, reaching 48 before falling to Rangana Herath, but helped Rooty add 89 on his way to a magnificent unbeaten 200. Sri Lanka batted well and I had the satisfaction that my first Test wicket was Kumar Sangakkara, one of the great batsmen of our times and a very nice, thoughtful man, although by then he had made 147. We thought we had won the match for at 6.42 on the final evening, Nuwan Pradeep edged forward to Broady, the ball went to Chris Jordan at second slip but on the half-volley, we appealed for lbw and the finger went up. The crowd roared. Cooky at slip thought he heard two sounds, Fernando asked for a review and that showed a thin inside edge. None of us knew what this draw would mean for the series.

That first Test had shown how the man with the beard had been accepted. I prayed five times a day as I always do and there was no problem. When I had sips of water on the field I knelt down in the way the Prophet had done. And when the Test ended and the singing and the drinks flowed, I left. I was Mo, the man with the beard, but I felt just as much a part of the England team as the others.

This was the first time I really got to know Jimmy Anderson. I enjoyed my banter with him about football, but with his beloved Burnley then seemingly stuck in the Championship, Jimmy didn't much like to hear about the mighty Reds.

Jimmy and I didn't have much chance to chat about football when exactly nine days later in Leeds, with about an hour and a half left of the second Test, he joined me to try to save the match. We had actually got a 109-run lead but allowed Sri Lanka to recover from 277 for 7 to 457. Cooky decided the way to get them all out was to give Mathews, who was batting well, a single so we could get at Herath. Cooky didn't bring me on despite the fact that earlier in the innings I had got Sangakkara again, this time for 55 and their number five, Chandika Thirimanne, for 0, which meant he got a pair. I finally came on, to sarcastic cheers from the Leeds crowd, and I nearly got Herath lbw and then Matt Prior dropped him when, as he swept, the ball ballooned off Herath's back pad. I did help get Mathews out, catching him off Jimmy, but by then he had made 160 and they were 437 for 9. They eventually set us a target of 350 and at the end of the fourth day's play we looked doomed at 57 for 5, with Cooky and Belly both out and only Rooty still there. Pundits freely speculated that no team in cricket history had ever saved a Test going into the final day with five wickets down but I'd been playing in that sort of situation throughout the summer and the season before for Worcester and that evening I told my brother Kadeer, 'Actually no matter what happens we can't win the game, but I'm not going to get out tomorrow. I'll be as solid as I can.'

Jimmy joined me with 81 minutes left of the match. A century beckoned but my main objective was to save the match and I had faith in Jimmy's batting, which was to prove its worth in the next Test against India at Nottingham when he got 81 and drove the Indians to despair. I got my hundred, but the celebrations had to be low-key as there was a bigger job that had to be done, saving the game. For the first time in my life I didn't feel like I was going to get out, I was so focussed and so determined. With six balls remaining in the match, Jimmy had been playing Herath well, so we decided he could face the last over. They brought Eranga back but I was not worried as Jimmy had played him with confidence.

Throughout the over, between balls, I kept talking to Jimmy, saying, 'One more ball, one more ball, just the next ball is the most important ball.' But he was very calm and I was not worried until that fifth ball. Eranga bowled one short and Jimmy, who had been taking it on his body, threw up his hands and was caught by Herath. It was, I must, say, a very good delivery. I had scored my first hundred for England in only my second Test but I was gutted. In a team game, whatever you do as an individual must always rank below what your team does. To be just two balls away from saving a Test and not doing it was awful. It also meant we lost the two-Test series.

However, the summer was to prove how fortunes in cricket can change. Mine certainly did. We came to Lord's for the second Test against India feeling bullish, having had much the better of the draw on a Trent Bridge wicket that was as flat as I have ever seen. Of that innings at Leeds against Sri Lanka *Wisden* would write, 'Dubbed, "The Beard That's Feared" by his county Worcestershire, he was far more than a marketing gimmick. This was a masterclass in technique and tempera-ment, with the wider context always taking priority over personal success.' But now on the final day of the Lord's Test I was told I could not face short-pitched bowling.

Rooty and I had come together on the fourth evening with the score 72 for 4 and by the close had taken it to 105 for 4. We required 319 to win, exactly what we had scored in the first innings, and as we neared lunch on the final day Rooty and I were still together.

Rooty and I were playing quite well. I was confident. I had done just the same against Sri Lanka trying to save the match and felt this time we could win. I thought we had a chance as long as we both stayed in. I didn't feel I was going to get out and Rooty was obviously playing really well. But Rooty at the time wasn't as good as he is now, he didn't have all those runs in the bank which can make such a difference. Our target was now below 150; these landmarks are important when you are chasing. Then just before lunch Ishant Sharma came on. Dhoni and he had a chat and Dhoni persuaded him to bowl at me round the wicket. I went down the wicket and had a chat with Rooty and I said, 'Rooty, what do you think? Shall I take it on, or shall I just ride the short ball?' Rooty said, 'Just play the way you have been playing.' There was a bit of doubt in my head, and because of that lack of clarity I got myself into a terrible position. The last ball before lunch he got me with a short ball which I gloved to Pujara at short-leg. That was the first time where I thought, right, I need to work on the short ball. Before that, throughout my whole career I'd never felt I had a problem when I faced Harmison, Malinga and other quick bowlers, and Sharma is not quick. He's tall. What he gets is a bit of bounce.

I also realized how Test cricket is different to county cricket. Not only are more people watching you but there are so many pundits putting the spotlight on what you do. If that happened in county cricket you'd probably turn around quickly, whereas in Test cricket people are talking. The spotlight is on you. That's actually very hard to deal with. After what was said about me at Lord's I felt I needed to work on how to cope with such criticism. It plays on your mind actually. I was very good in my first few years at just putting the media to one side to carry on working hard. Once you come into Test cricket you realize how big it is. County cricket does not prepare you for that leap into Test cricket. It is on television. Everybody's analysing the game and talking about your technique. People are saying you can't play this, you can't play that. England's performances are on the ten o'clock news and the front pages of the newspapers. With newspapers having sports supplements now there is a lot written about Test cricket. In comparison county cricket hardly gets a mention and some papers do not even print score cards. In that first summer playing for England I realized that I would have to adjust to this intense scrutiny for the rest of my career and get used to the criticism. I was fortunate in that being an all-rounder, my bowling was taking the spotlight off my batting.

And behind the scenes at Lord's I was getting help with my bowling. Cooky encouraged me with my spin. Belly told me to bowl quicker and even the umpire in the Test, Kumar Dharmasena, played a huge part. In practice sessions for two days before the Test Dharmasena happened to be there umpiring in the nets, which umpires do to get their eye in. They even call no-ball if a bowler has overstepped the mark in the nets.

During the Trent Bridge Test standing at square leg I used to talk a lot to Kumar Dharmasena about his playing career, and how many games he's played. Just trying to make conversation with him. We slowly got onto bowling. He told me he liked my style of bowling. He said I've got a natural curve on the ball. I said to him, 'I feel like I need to bowl a bit quicker but I don't know how to bowl quicker without bowling flat.' He said, 'I'm going to come to the nets at Lord's and I'll teach you.' So when he came I reminded him. I said to Kumar, 'You were a spinner. You played with Murali and all those guys. How do I try and bowl quicker? I need to bowl quicker in Test cricket and one-day cricket.'

We spoke over the two days of the nets. I found that when it comes to spin bowling the subcontinental cultures are very different to our English culture. The English guys would say, my left arm being my sort of direction arm, pull that down quickly and pull it to my hip almost. But Kumar simply said to me, 'With your left hand, grab your left pocket as quick as you can. Do everything exactly the same, just with that arm grab your pocket. So as soon as you get your left arm high to get ready to bowl, grab the pocket as quick as you can.'

He then demonstrated how to do it. And then he told me about my back leg, with my follow through, it's like your car windscreen wipers. 'Remember that arc in your back leg, it has to be like the windscreen wipers.' They use that kind of imagery in the subcontinent rather than what we are told about driving the leg through or up. It's a different way of coaching. You cannot have the same coaching for every person.

That was the best advice on spin bowling I have ever received.

At the Lord's game I felt that I bowled well. I took two wickets. I had Kohli dropped – Prior dropped him, it was a thin nick – and then I got Stuart Binny and Ravindra Jadeja out, and overall I bowled really tight. It was the first time in Test cricket I bowled tight. So I got confidence from that and I thought, Now just try and be accurate. At Trent Bridge I'd taken four wickets on a pitch that was really slow and low. The match referee David Boon said it was a 'poor pitch', only the third time the ICC had classified a pitch that way. As early as the first afternoon Steve Birks, the head groundsman, was issuing something which was very nearly an apology with Nottinghamshire chief executive Lisa Pursehouse denying the pitch had been prepared to last five days. You can judge how the pitch was from the fact that for the first time in Test cricket both England and India put on 100 for the tenth wicket and both number elevens, Bhuvneshwar Kumar and Jimmy Anderson, scored 50s. But I was going for runs. At Lord's on debut, I had got Sangakkara out. Headingley, I got Sangakkara out. So I knew I was picking up wickets, but I wasn't bowling tight enough. And in county cricket before that I was getting good players out most of the time, but still conceding runs.

It all came right at the Southampton Test a week after Lord's. For very different reasons both Cooky and I were under scrutiny. The pressure on Cooky was due to his batting.

The media was relentlessly reminding him he had not scored a century in fourteen Tests, nor had England won a Test in that period. Cooky never said anything. He doesn't say a lot in response to that sort of criticism. With his game you never know if he's in good form or bad form. He's that sort of guy. He's just always the same. On the first morning we batted first and, on 15, he edged Pankaj Singh, a 6ft 6in bowler, a big Sikh guy who had come in for the injured Sharma, and Jadeja dropped a regulation catch at slip. Had Cooky been caught it could have been a different game. I could see he was under pressure. He came off for lunch still batting and he got a big cheer because he was 50 not out and I remember him saying how much that cheer from the crowd meant to him. Everyone was happy and for Cooky it was almost like a massive burden off his shoulders. He was close to resigning at that time.

I was under pressure for different reasons.

During the Test while batting in the first innings I had worn wristbands saying 'Free Palestine' and 'Save Gaza'. The ICC reprimanded me but the ECB to their credit stood by me and saw it as the humanitarian gesture it was meant to be and not remotely political. I had worn it thinking of the words of Nelson

Mandela at the gates of my primary school, 'We know too well that our freedom is incomplete without the freedom of the Palestinians.' How could anyone not agree with what the greatest man of our times has said? When I wore the wristbands I didn't really know it was going to be such a big deal.

But it generated dreadful controversy. I got letters, nasty ones, which had death threats. Some were sent to me at the ground. Some were sent to Worcester. The MCC got letters. Some were printed out. Some were written by hand. I was also sent articles about terrorism and all that kind of stuff. So when I got to bowling in the Indian innings, after we had made 569 for 7 declared, I felt I was under pressure to perform in that game.

I came on to bowl when the Indians were going well. Rohit Sharma and Ajinkya Rahane, who had scored a hundred at Lord's, were batting well and they had got to 210 for 4. Then just before tea Sharma came down the track to me, completely misjudged the flight, got nowhere near the pitch and Broady at mid-off did the rest. Seven runs later I got Rahane. Okay, it was a half tracker, but you do get wickets with bad balls and he toe-ended it to Terry, who had come on as sub at mid-on.

We didn't enforce the follow-on. Cooky, now full of confidence, made a measured 70 not out and we set the Indians 445 or go for a draw, facing out 132 overs. Cooky brought me on early, they were 26 for 1 and Pujara edged my second ball. It seemed to have gone past Chris Jordan at slip and it was travelling, but he held on to it. If any Indian could stick around it was Pujara. I also had Kohli caught behind. To get Pujara and

Kohli was, obviously, a massive boost for me. By stumps on the fourth day India were 112 for 4, with Rahane and Sharma, both good players of spin, still there. So there was work to do. But by 12.48 on the last day I had bowled Pankaj Singh, the match was over, we had won by 266 runs and the pre-lunch session had seen wickets tumbling so quickly that they had opened the gates and let the crowds in free. To take 6 for 67 in 20.4 overs, two of India's main batsmen and numbers eight, nine, ten and eleven, including Jadeja and Kumar, both of whom can bat, was a wonderful feeling. Three of them were bowled and there is nothing like getting a wicket when you beat a batsman and the ball hits the stumps.

Did the Indians take me a bit casually? Maybe they treated me with a sort of 'Well, he is only an English spinner and we from the subcontinent are masters of playing spin. That is our dal and roti, bread and butter.' I'm guessing because our seamers have been so good, most teams would attack me seeing me as the weak link and that obviously can play to my advantage.

The Southampton Test was a big one for me, in terms of believing in my bowling a bit more, especially when the batting wasn't going as well as I would have liked. But the biggest thing was that the Southampton game was the first time I realized that I'd done something to win the game. I'd actually done something for England. Now I felt as if I belonged and now I could try and take my career forward. I could obviously do it with a bat because I had got a hundred and then I got six wickets. Six wickets and a century in my first six games and I thought, 'You know what, having waited so long you can do this, you can actually play Test cricket.'

Then the next game at Old Trafford I got four wickets as well. That was a seaming wicket and it had a bit of bounce. Jimmy and Broady were unplayable in the first innings and cleaned them up – I was not required to bowl. In the second innings my four wickets were Pujara, Rahane, Dhoni and Jadeja. The Indians didn't know whether to slog me or play defensively and we won by an innings and 54 runs. We were even more dominant in the Oval Test where we won in three days by an innings and 244 runs. Jimmy, Broady and the two Chrisses (Jordan and Woakes) were so commanding that I bowled only one over in the entire match. I finished the series with 19 wickets, as many as Broady, and as the cricketing experts told me later, you had to go back to Ray Illingworth in 1967 to find an English spinner taking more wickets against India in a home series.

I even got to open the bowling for England, in the Twenty20 international. I got the first Indian wicket, bowling Rahane on 3. I must say a brand new ball is quite difficult, most of the time it's going to skid. I prefer to come on after, say, 8 or 10 overs, especially if there's a bit of spin for me.

I played in one of the one-day internationals, a series we lost 3-1, and in the only Twenty20, which we won by three runs. Both my matches were in my home town, Birmingham. In the one-day international I decided the only way to cope with the Indian spinners, Ashwin, Jadeja and Raina, was to use my feet and get to the pitch of the bowling, and got to my 50 in 37 balls. I eventually made 67 but every time I sallied forth to hit them the crowd booed. This booing was repeated five days later when at the same ground we played the Twenty20 match. Even when I was fielding, every time the ball came to me and my name got called out they just booed me. I reckon at both the Birmingham matches 80 per cent of the crowd were Indian supporters. The most disappointing thing was that it was my home ground – I was born and raised in Birmingham. These supporters who were booing me would have been from here as well, probably, most of them.

What made the booing all the more puzzling was that I have a huge fan base in India and when I played in the IPL in the spring of 2018 there was no question of being booed. In India the fans are different.

I have been asked whether the Indians in Birmingham felt that I was somehow betraying them because my heritage is Pakistani, even though I am representing England. Maybe there is something in that. Prior to this I had heard from former players who have played for England, Asian players, that they got abuse from the Pakistani fans, or the Indian fans, depending on whether they are of Indian or Pakistani origin, being called a traitor or whatever. But I always felt that actually I was representing these people more than anything. It is interesting that when we played Pakistan it was completely different, it was the total opposite; the support I got from the fans in this country playing against Pakistan was amazing. Every time I came out or my name was announced, the crowd would be singing, 'He's one of us.' You appreciate that a lot. I think the Indians in the crowd probably thought of the problems between India and Pakistan and because I was doing so well against India at the time they did not like it. Maybe by booing me they were trying to put me off – an English spinner was taking wickets against their heroes who were supposed to be the world's best players of spin bowling.

At Birmingham the England boys did ask me, 'Do you want us to say something to the umpires and we can get them kicked out.' I said no. Part of it is what happens when people drink, as you don't know half the time what you're doing or saying which is the reason why we Muslims don't drink. My reaction showed how much I had changed and matured. Four or five years before such booing would have probably made me quite angry. By this time I had been booed a bit and had come to accept that in the end they feel it's their right to say what they want and they boo because they can.

The Indian series was interesting because it showed the very different attitude Indian supporters have to Test cricket as opposed to the one-day game. The ECB was assuming that Indians would turn up for the Test matches but they didn't because they don't follow Test cricket. They turned up for the one-day matches. Only in England, Australia and South Africa will people turn up for Test matches. It's the same story in India: crowds turn up in droves for the one-day matches, but there's no interest in the Tests. In England home Tests are packed out most of the time and we get a lot of kids attending. We're very, very fortunate in that.

The series was also important for me in terms of my relationship with the coach. In contrast to my non-existent relationship with Ashley Giles, I had struck up a wonderful rapport with Peter Moores. Billy, to use his nickname, was in charge for his first series at home, a proper series. Billy has had his critics. Kevin Pietersen had a fairly public disagreement with him. But he is a fantastic coach. He has proved that winning county championships with two different counties, Lancashire and Sussex, and he won two trophies in 2017, his first year with Nottingham.

Billy was brilliant with me and always encouraged me to do my best. What makes him such an amazing coach is how he handles his players. If you're coming into the team for the first time or if you're a youngster, Billy never lets you feel uncomfortable or like you don't fit in. When you come in sometimes you feel you're probably not working as hard as you would like. He's good at driving you and trying to get the best out of you. For me he was brilliant at pushing me, saying I've got more to go.

That series with India established me in the public eye. The legend of the beard had already started at Worcester. Even before I finally got the England call my performances in county cricket made Worcester followers print shirts with my face showing my beard and imprinted on it, 'The Beard that's Feared'. When I was doing well it was all over social media. It was following the Southampton Test that this got pushed out a lot more to the entire country.

My comment that I was wearing a beard because it represented my faith did provoke criticism. This is what historian Arunabha Sengupta wrote about it on the DNA India website:

Moeen Ali's personal choice of sporting a beard for religious considerations has managed to stir a hornet's nest. Some journalists, specifically Michael Henderson of the *Telegraph*, have taken issue with his proclamation that his beard was like a uniform, a label representing the Muslim faith.

Rather curiously, the chief argument against Moeen has been that as a member of the national team he could represent only one thing – the country he played for. And somewhat more curiously, Henderson wrote that the 'uniform' was the symbol of equality irrespective of financial status, political inclination or ethnicity, and 'a man who belongs to a team and draws attention to his beard as a symbol of his faith is opting to stand out'. [...]

In some ways, the question asked by the journalist was rhetorical. Everyone knows the reason behind a beard of such dimensions. It represents a particular faith, and that is all there is to it. Whether it is Saqlain Mushtaq, Saeed Anwar, Mohammad Yousuf, Hashim Amla or Moeen Ali sporting one, it is indeed a symbol of faith. And seldom has the outgrowth come between a cricketer and his performances or his loyalty.

Hashim Amla admittedly did not proclaim he was representing people of the Islamic faith by sporting his beard, perhaps because no one asked. As long as his strokes were as luxurious as his beard, no one complained. But it did not stop Dean Jones from branding him a terrorist in a stage whisper – which was unfortunately caught on the micro-phone. The beard is that obvious, everyone knows what it stands for. [...]

This is not the first time a cricketer has flaunted his faith on the cricket field ... Both Wes Hall and Dennis Lillee charged in with their intimidating deliveries while their cru-cifixes dangled from their necks and swung like crazy pen-dulums.... [T]hey could not have denied they were devout Christians who carried their faith with them. If this caused them to 'stand out in the dressing room', none of their teammates complained. Neither did the Indians have any issue with Bishan Bedi's colourful patka, even if he 'stood out' in every team photograph because of the trappings of his faith.

What about Viv Richards and his Rastafarian wristbands of green, yellow and red? He batted for West Indies and proudly represented his African brothers. If we look at the battered and bruised bowlers of the day, it did not matter much that his wristbands eloquently proclaimed that he represented more than just his team on the field. [...]

As long as he [excels at the game], the way he sports his beard, and the reasons that contribute to the sustenance and shape of vegetation on his chin, should not be any-one's concern but his own. It will perhaps be best for the game if the media stopped splitting hairs about this trivial issue.[1]

It was good to read this measured piece that usefully put the issue into historical context. What really comforted me was that, unlike my critics, the English fans understood why I had a beard and why it should not be seen as alien let alone a threat. That it should instead be celebrated as part of the diverse Britain that has emerged. The Beard that's Feared went national in the 2014 season as I was now part of England. Nobody could question that.

1 http://www.dnaindia.com/analysis/standpoint-there-is-nothing-objectionable-if-england-s-moeen-ali-chooses-to-represent-his-faith-by-sporting-his-beard-1995833

CHAPTER 10

A WORLD CUP HORROR STORY

E ngland never do well in World Cups. We launched the tournament. The first three were all held in England and we have been to three finals, once when it was a 60-over tournament, and lost all three. In fact the last time England was in a final I was four years old. So, you could say it was ridiculous to expect much from the World Cup in Australia and New Zealand in February–March 2015. It was meticulously planned but then we shot ourselves in the foot just before the tournament started. And then further messed it up before a ball was bowled in the first match.

The self-harm happened as a result of playing a pre-Christmas one-day-international tour of Sri Lanka. It was meant to give us the sort of preparation that planners thought would make a smooth transition for the trip Down Under.

For me the trip could not have gone better – I've said before how much I love going to Sri Lanka. I had been brought in to replace Alex Hales because I was an all-rounder and I was asked to open. In the first warm-up match, in the second over of the innings, Cooky having faced the first, I hit left-armer Vishwa Fernando for six fours. He also bowled a wide which meant we got 25 runs from the over. I reached my 50 in 21 balls and Cooky and I put on 94 in 13 overs. So I went into the opening ODI in Colombo full of spirit. Chasing 317, I played, said the press, in the style that the two great Lankan heroes, Sanath Jayasuriya and Romesh Kaluwitharana, had shown when Sri Lanka won the World Cup in 1996. My century came in 72 balls, the third fastest hundred by an England batsman in this format. I made 119 from 87 balls, with eleven fours and five sixes, all of them on the leg-side, and plundered 38 from 16 balls bowled by Sri Lankan opener Dhammika Prasad.

What really pleased me about this innings was that for the first time I really felt I showed England how I can play. Before that I had done it in bits and bobs. In playing for England I had been boxed in to play less attacking cricket, as if I was a defensive number seven or eight, a grafter who can shore up an innings when the side is in trouble. But that has never been my game. I was brought up as an attacking batsman. The *Wisden* correspondent described it as 'an innings that combined beauty and the beast'. But apart from Ravi Bopara who made 65, no one else contributed and we lost by 25 runs.

We lost the second game but in the third at Hambantota chasing 242 I got to my half century in 29 balls, with four sixes. The first of these had come when Prasad had bowled one short outside the off-stump and I freed my arms and hit a square drive that went over the ropes. I hit another six and then, on 58, and because of one of those classic mix-ups, I was run out. But Jos Buttler made sure we did not squander what had been built. As it was, we won only one more match, losing the seven-match series 5-2.

Poor Cooky had a dreadful time. At Hambantota, he and I had put on 84 in 12 overs. But the 34 he made there was Cooky's highest score and this meant he had made just one 50 in 22 one-day innings since June 2013. We returned less than a week before Christmas and it was announced Cooky would not be taking the team to the World Cup. Eoin Morgan would take over. This could have been handled better, with news leaking out before James Whittaker could contact Morgy, who was playing in the Big Bash in Australia.

But it was also a mistake. I actually think Cooky would have done all right in the World Cup. The wickets there suited him. He wouldn't have scored big but he would have done quite well.

I had, of course, every reason to feel happy as we headed Down Under. The critics were unanimous that I had made a striking impact. As part of our preparation we had a tri-series against Australia and India and beat India twice. In the first match India were bowled out for 153, their lowest score against England ever, and I got the wicket of Suresh Raina. In the second win at Perth I got the wickets of Kohli and Raina in the space of 4 runs. We did lose to Australia, including in the final in Perth, and it was clear we would have to sharpen up before the World Cup began, our opening match being against Australia in Melbourne exactly fourteen days later.

But this is where the wheels started coming off. We had a set batting order prior to the World Cup. But when the first game arrived, James Taylor moved from number three to number six. Gary Ballance got picked and batted number three. The bowling order changed, with Woakesy, who had opened in all our tri-series matches with Jimmy Anderson or Steven Finn, now brought on as first change with Broady, who was the number-three bowler, opening with Jimmy. I don't know who made all the changes. I don't think it was Morgy, who had just taken over the captaincy. I couldn't believe that we needed to make so many changes. I suspect Morgy wasn't happy either. He was prepared to take over as captain but it was not his team and he had to cope with the management structure that was already in place. Peter Moores was in charge and Mark Ramprakash was the batting coach. As can often happen, the fifth ball of the match poor Woakesy dropped a simple catch at square-leg when Aaron Finch flicked Jimmy. He went on to make 135 and the result was that in the very first game we played, Australia, in front of a raucous 90,000 crowd packing the day-night match, scored 342. My figures of 0 for 60 were the tightest figures out of everybody. We were that bad. We got rolled over for 231. Poor Taylor, demoted to number six, ran out of partners and was 98 not out at the end; the next highest scorer was Woakes with 37. It showed that when you make sudden changes it just does not pay off.

It got even worse at Wellington where, batting first on a wicket that exploited swing and seam, New Zealand's Tim Southee destroyed us, bowling us out for 123. I was one of his seven victims and my 20 was the second highest score after Rooty's

46. Before lunch was even taken they needed 12 to win. It was that embarrassing. I did get into the groove against Scotland at Christchurch, scoring 128 in 107 balls, hitting five sixes, and my stand with Ian Bell of 172 was England's best in World Cups. Belly was more sedate, his 54 coming in 85 balls. Fair enough it was Scotland but these days there are no minnows.

It was when we played Sri Lanka in our next match at Wellington that I found my philosophy of one-day cricket did not chime with the views of the one-day management team. We had won the toss, batted, and after 9 overs Belly and I had put on 61 for the first wicket. Our template was to get 50 for 0 after ten. So we were ahead of our schedule. I felt it was such a good wicket, a small boundary, that we needed more than what our template said. I decided we needed to accelerate and got caught at mid-off the next over off Mathews. I got out feeling that I had tried to do the right thing. As I walked off Peter Moores called me over and for the first time he had a go at me for getting out the way I did. I said, 'Look, I felt it was a better wicket. We could score more.' My point was templates need to be adjusted as a match progresses. You may have a set plan but you must be ready to change if the situation is different. You have to adapt. In that match thanks to a brilliant 121 by Rooty we got to 309 but Sri Lanka came out and won by nine wickets in 47.2 overs. Sangakkara scored an unbelievable 117 from 70 balls, the fastest of his career. I managed to get Dilshan out, our only wicket, but we had been blown away, absolutely destroyed. That made me realize that actually the way I was going about it was right, even though it was against the template.

Even before we lost against Bangladesh there was no doubt the World Cup in Australia had been a disaster.

The fact was the Test team and the one-day team were too similar with too many familiar faces and we badly needed the revamp which took place after that World Cup.

The day after we were dumped out of the tournament we had a team meeting in our Sydney hotel to discuss why things had gone so badly. Everybody had to say what they thought and we went round the room listening to each other's opinions.

I didn't want to say too much. I'd just got into the team but I said I felt maybe our skill level was not as good as everybody else's. The other teams were playing shots and putting on big scores and we were still a little bit behind – *way* behind. Before the World Cup the management had set out the template that we should score 280 runs if we batted first. That score would be a platform for victory. But as we found in Australia, one-day cricket had changed: 280 was not a winning score. You needed 300 plus. But then a few other people spoke and the strangest contribution was from Ravi Bopara. He had told me beforehand he was not going to speak up at all. But when the meeting got underway he could not have been more vociferous, saying, 'You guys are bringing me down ... I can't play with you guys' and all that kind of stuff.

The one good thing about the World Cup was we did change our white-ball one-day philosophy. Moores went.

Morgy officially became the captain and he was the guy who really shaped the one-day team. It completely changed. He brought in the players that he wanted. He, Trevor Bayliss and Paul 'Farby' Farbrace, who were now the coaches, really got together and changed our whole approach to playing white-ball cricket. That's when we started on the right track. Morgy's theory was we must try and almost hit the lights out when we're batting and really go for it, always taking the positive option. You are taking a risk; you could get out to a bad shot, holing out at the deep mid-wicket boundary. That's fine, just do it better next time. What he said was exactly what I wanted to hear. Now Farby and everyone started telling me, 'You know, actually we need everybody to play like you do.' I was also enthusiastic about playing under Morgy. He is probably the best captain I've played under, so calm. It's just amazing the way he captains the side. There are times when a team under pressure gets tired and everyone's throwing their arms about in panic but he's calm. The calmest on the ground.

I had not played in our final match against Afghanistan, having picked up a side strain, but I returned from the World Cup pretty happy. There's no circumstances in which your only victories coming against Scotland and Afghanistan can be considered remotely satisfactory but from the ruins had emerged the glimmer of hope.

CHAPTER 11

TAKE THAT, OSAMA

like to think I am a calm person. I can take most things in my stride. It was the night of 7 July 2015. I was in our Cardiff hotel where the next day England were due to play Australia in the first Ashes Test of the summer and for the first time in my life I was nervous about playing cricket. I really wanted to do well. I knew everyone was watching. I didn't have to be told how big the series was. If you are English and love cricket you know what the Ashes mean. The Aussies were a good side. We actually believed that we could beat them. I did my prayers and then I tried to sleep. But through the night I was just spinning, tossing and turning. I had never had such a restless night before a cricket match. Eventually I did drop off and when I woke up at around 8 or 8.30 I was ready to go.

I felt even more relaxed when I got to the Swalec stadium and the ground started filling up with spectators. The Cardiff crowd proved amazing throughout the match. Nothing calms your nerves more than playing in front of a good cricket crowd who know the game, who are loud and always cheering you on. By the time we won the toss and decided to bat I was more my normal self and ready for my first Ashes encounter. Normally, when we bat I like to have a snooze, but the way wickets were falling I was not sure when I might be needed; we were three down for 43 and might have been four down as Rooty was dropped off his second ball by Brad Haddin. But he made the most of it, got a 134 and I went in with the score 292 for 6. Stokesy had just got out to Mitchell Starc and I was clear in my mind what I would do. I went two, two, two, off Starc's first three balls. Nathan Lyon was bowling from the other end. Since our first meeting at Cardiff much has been made of my duels with Lyon and, in particular, how I faced him in Australia in the winter of 2017. But in my first encounter with him in a Test, the very first ball he bowled me I hit for six. I had decided I would always go after him and he never got me once in that series. Just before the close Jos Buttler got out and Broady joined me and by the end of the first day's play we'd moved on to 343 for 7 with me on 26 and Broady yet to score. That night I slept well and I was feeling confident the next morning as Broady and I walked out with the Cardiff crowd cheering us to the rafters.

As I made my way to the middle I reminded myself of my philosophy in such a scenario. Bat properly until Broady comes into bat. Then when he comes in we both hit out, or we get out. Throughout that series when we were batting together – and we often did, having a stand of some proportion in all but one of the five Tests – we would meet in the middle and say to each other, 'There is no in between.' This was because we knew that this would bring the best out of us both. I knew that Broady couldn't really hang around against the quicks or the spinners, so at least if he's going to get out, he gets out blazing away. Starting that second morning at Cardiff we established a pattern of meeting in the middle when we were batting and trying to see who can out-hit each other. To me it made perfect sense. If you can get runs in this manner for the seventh- or eighth-wicket partnerships it can be very demoralizing for the opposition, taking the momentum away from them before we go in and bowl. It also helped that I have never had any problems running between the wickets with Broady. Our under-standing of when to run was excellent.

We also took into consideration that Michael Clarke was an attacking captain. He doesn't do what other captains would probably do in that situation and put a sweeper back to guard the boundaries. That gave us the licence to just swing the bat as hard as we could.

The 77 I made that morning was my second highest score for England at that stage and when I was ninth out we had reached 419; our final total of 430 batting first was a score Cooky would have taken when he decided to bat.

I was also very pleased when I was brought on to bowl and about the way Cooky used me. Just as I had targeted Lyon, Steve Smith targeted me, hitting three of my first four balls for fours. But Cooky did not take me off, and instead positioned himself at short-leg. I saw Smith coming down the wicket and sent the ball down the leg-side. Smith, worried he might be stumped, got totally confused and popped a catch to Cooky at short-leg. I also caught and bowled Clarke and with our pacers chipping in, taking the other eight wickets, we had a handy lead of 122. We were batting before lunch on the third day. Cooky fell early and before play resumed after lunch we had evidence of the new England thinking for Test cricket. For the first time since he had taken over as coach Trevor Bayliss spoke properly to the team. There was still a lot of time left in the Test. We had a very tricky batting session coming up, it was overcast and I know in the past we would have tried to survive this spell. But Bayliss said this was not about survival. This was about scoring runs. We needed to attack. We took him at his word. Ian Bell and Adam Lyth added 41 in one 20-ball sequence, we all swung our bat and, although by the close of play we were bowled out, we had a lead of 411 and six sessions to bowl the Aussies out.

We got Chris Rogers out cheaply but the other Australians batted well. I must say they had us worried. There was a bit of spin but I didn't feel I was bowling strongly. In 2 overs I went for 22. But by the time I bowled the final over before lunch, I'd found my rhythm. I bowled three dot balls to David Warner which he played defensively, obviously looking to the lunch break, and then with the fourth ball I had him lbw.

After lunch I got Haddin with Cooky taking a brilliant catch at short midwicket, leaping to his right, first palming the ball down, then clinging on to stop it falling to the ground. Best of all I intervened after Mitchell Johnson, crashing the ball to all parts in making 77, their highest score, looked like he might hold us up. I got the last wicket, that of Josh Hazlewood, just before the end of the fourth day's play. We had won by 169 runs.

Jimmy congratulating me following my first Test wicket: Kumar Sangakkara at Lord's, June 2014.

Celebrating the wicket of M.S. Dhoni in the fourth Test against India, Old Trafford, 2014.

It was an absolute honour to be one of Wisden's Cricketers of the Year in 2014.

The fifth day of the First Test against New Zealand, 2015 – one of the best matches I've played in at Lord's.

I was very nervous about playing my first Ashes Test in 2015, but having Rash in the squad made a big difference.

A brilliant start to the opening Ashes Test in 2015 for England, and for me personally, taking the wicket of Michael Clarke.

Banging one past Stokesy in training as I always do.

After a win in the Durban Test in 2015, I took Abu Bakr onto the field and let him have a run around.

Singing the national anthem with Cooky, Rooty and Bluey at Wanderers Stadium, January 2016.

In Johannesburg with the best captain I've ever played under, Eoin Morgan.

Enjoying a charity event playing football with the locals in Nyanga Township in Cape Town.

Back in Sparkhill for a Chance to Shine event – just checking to see if I've still got it in the box!

Scoring my 100th goal in training and awarding myself the Golden Boot.

Playing IPL for the Royal Challengers Bangalore, one of the best experiences I've had in cricket. It was a real honour to call players like Virat Kohli and Mohammed Siraj teammates.

My parents. I can never thank them enough for everything they've done for me.

With Firuza and Abu Bakr at home.

Me and my beautiful mother, the person who is dearest to me.

It was a great first Ashes Test in terms of my personal performance, however there was one incident which had distracted me. An Australian player had turned to me on the field and said 'Take that, Osama.' I could not believe what I had heard. I remember going really red. I have never been so angry on a cricket field. I told a couple of the guys what the player had said to me and I think Trevor must have raised it with Darren Lehmann, the Australians' coach. Lehmann asked the player, 'Did you call Moeen Osama?' He denied it, saying, 'No, I said, "Take that, you part-timer."' I must say I was amused when I heard that for there is a world of difference between the words 'Osama' and 'part-timer'. Although I couldn't have mistaken 'part-timer' for 'Osama', obviously I had to take the player's word for it, though for the rest of the match I was angry.

But our eventual triumph and the Cardiff crowd's reaction to me comforted me that the Australian player represented nobody. English – and indeed Welsh – crowds considered me English not some foreign alien. I was as central to the England team as the rest of the lads who had just beaten the Aussies.

However, Cardiff did make me, and all of us in the England team, realize how different these 2015 Australians were. Normally after a match the two teams fraternize, whatever the result. It is a sporting contest. You have fought hard. But you respect each other. You recognize that in a match there will be a winner and a loser and the tradition is after the game you mingle, go to each other's dressing room, a fortress during the match but after it an open house for good-natured banter between professionals earning a living playing a game they love. The great majority of people spend their entire lives doing work they don't enjoy. But they have to, to put bread on the table. We as cricketers know we earn money doing something that we have wanted to do since childhood. The picture of Freddie Flintoff comforting Brett Lee after England had beaten Australia at Edgbaston in the epic 2005 Ashes series has gone down in history. So have Freddie's immortal words, 'I was taught as a kid always respect the opposition first and celebrate after, which I did. I went over to Brett Lee and shook his hand and there's that picture, where I whisper in his ear: "It's 1-1, son."'

But we discovered at Cardiff that the 2015 Aussies did not share this attitude. For whatever reason they were just not talking to us. Not only during the game but even on the training days before the Test started. Their coaching staff wouldn't come to our coaching staff. At the end of the Test we went out of our way to reach out to them and after we had won we invited them over to our dressing room. We wanted to see what their reaction would be. To our amazement they said no, they didn't want to come. Some of the lads wanted to actually force our way into their dressing room. This led to a bit of debate. We decided not to do that in the end, to wait until the end of the series. One member of their squad, Fawad Ahmed, a leg-spinner who knows my brother quite well, told him that they were not allowed to speak to us. It was crazy. I don't know why they adopted this attitude. Maybe they wanted to show that they were here just to focus on the cricket and not to make friends. Yes, you want to win but for me that is not the attitude to take. That devalues sport. The Australian cricketers have always believed that when you play the game you must be in the face of your opposition. To them to be a runner-up is not a consolation but denotes the first loser. Fair enough, you want to win and play hard, but we don't have the mentality that the 2015 Aussies showed. I am glad we are not that sort of team. We want to win but we don't see a sporting contest as a war.

I came to Lord's feeling good about my cricket and with warm memories of my previous visit six weeks earlier when we had played New Zealand. During that game, old timers who knew Lord's intimately had told me they had never seen such an atmosphere at the home of cricket. In that match against the Kiwis I scored 58 in the first innings and took three wickets in their first including that of Kane Williamson and opener Tom Latham. The real drama came on the final day when the queues to get into Lord's went all the way down to St John's Wood station. The crowd were expecting England to press home for victory and Cooky and I got a tremendous roar as we resumed our second innings at 429 for 6. Cooky was on 153, I was on 19. We were 295 ahead but needed more before we could let New Zealand have a go. Cooky went quickly but I followed instructions to get quick runs and by the time I was ninth out for 43 we were 478. Jimmy didn't trouble the scorer and we set New Zealand a target of 345. More importantly we had 77 overs and felt we could bowl them out. But although we made early breakthroughs – they were 61 for 5 at one stage – their middle order proved stubborn and 9 overs after tea New Zealand were 168 for 5 and it looked like they might get away with a draw. But then Mark Wood broke the stand, Joe Root got Anderson, who with 67 was their top scorer, and when I ran into bowl I could hear the crowd shouting, 'bowled, bowled, bowled', much in the style of crowds in the subcontinent cheering their bowlers. I had never heard such encouragement before in England. I caught and bowled Southee and then caught Boult, who had taken my wickets in both innings, off Broady. The picture taken just after I took the catch summed up the mood brilliantly. I have both my arms raised and Stokesy, Rooty and Jos are running towards me to embrace me as they would a goalscorer, while in the pavilion members are on their feet cheering. The reception we got when we trooped back to the Long Room was so touching.

But in the endless see-saw that makes sport so fascinating, that wonderful memory of the spring bank holiday vanished at my very first net practice at Lord's and I very nearly didn't play in the Lord's Test. I was bowling in the nets at the Nursery End and I did my side. I felt it straightaway. It was very painful. I couldn't bowl the way I wanted to bowl. I thought there's no way I can play in this game. The physio knew it was a serious muscle injury. I had a scan. Normally it takes seven to ten days to heal, but the scan showed a grade one so it would probably be about two to four weeks. My mind was a riot of thoughts. This is the second game of the Ashes, I'm in good form and it's a good pitch. I need to keep playing. They phoned Adil Rashid. Rash had a bad finger and he said, 'I can't play, my finger's not a hundred per cent. If I'm playing I want to be a hundred per cent.' He hadn't played a Test match and I think he was a bit nervous, to be honest. So then Trevor Bayliss came up to me and said, 'Look, I know it's bad but we need you to play. Do you think you can get through?' I said, 'I probably can get through but I'll have to change my bowling action to try to compensate.' By this time I was also mentally prepared to play. Just before Trevor spoke to me I had walked down the steps of the pavilion and as I stepped onto the field I thought, you know what, this is a game I can't miss. Somehow I have to play this Test. Trevor further comforted me: 'Look, your adrenalin will get you through everything. Don't worry, you'll be fine.' My action normally is quite high and stretched but now I held myself in and tried not to lift my arm too high, not over my ear as I bowled. I was almost crouching and tensing my abs a bit. It was difficult. Trevor had helped me change my action and while it was not painful by the end of the match I was basically just getting through.

Cooky had to bring me on before lunch. The Aussies on winning the toss had batted so well that Rogers and Warner had put on a half-century opening stand. As at Cardiff Warner tried to smash me but with my fifth ball I had him caught by

Jimmy. But this brought Smith in. We did not get another wicket until well into the second day with Smith and Rogers putting on the highest Ashes partnership at Lord's. Smith got 215, Rogers 173 (on a ground he knows well), and all our predictions proved wrong. In trying to encourage me to play Trevor had said, 'You probably won't bowl much anyway because it's a good pitch and the seamers will do most of the bowling.' I ended up bowling 52 overs in the match, 36 in the first innings, more than Jimmy, Broady, Woody and almost twice as many as Stokesy. In the second innings I bowled another 16 overs, again got Warner out and also bowled Smith after he had made 58. In our first innings I got 39 and had another stand with Broady, but our 312 in reply to 566 was never going to be enough. Even then set 509 to win or bat five sessions, we got rolled over far too easily, did not even last two and were beaten by 405 runs.

There was the inevitable debate about England. Why, after winning so well at Cardiff, had we just collapsed at Lord's? So we turned up at my home ground at Edgbaston for the third Test with the talk all about how bad England were. One look at the ground and the conditions convinced me we should bowl. It was a bit of a green wicket, it was overcast but the team management had decided we were going to bat first. As I heard this I felt like shouting, 'No, no we can't bat, we need to bowl first.' I kept quiet but when Cooky lost the toss I punched the air. Never have I been so happy to lose the toss. What was also pleasing was that, like Cooky, Michael Clarke wanted to bat first as well. Of course, I didn't expect to bowl and I didn't need to. Jimmy, who had left Lord's without taking a wicket for the first time in eighteen Tests there, now had his best figures in an Ashes Test, 6 for 46; such are the ups and downs of this great game of ours. Australia were skittled out for 136. They didn't look the side they were at Lord's. As soon as the ball moved around they were nowhere near as good a team. As at Cardiff we had a bit of a middle-order collapse and 132 for 2 became 190 for 7. For the third successive Test Broady and I got together and piled on the runs, following the principles we had set at Cardiff.

I will never forget the crowd on that second afternoon at the ground where I learnt cricket. They were going wild as Broady and I batted. The Australians pitched it up and I drove while Broady was more of a carver of the Aussie attack. We were giving Mitchell Johnson a bit of stick. I hit him for three fours in three balls and the crowd was immediately on his back. The Barmy Army started singing, 'He bowls to the left, he bowls to the right, poor Mitchell Johnson, his bowling is shite.' It actually got to him and it clearly rattled the Australians. You could see in the body language when we were playing our shots that they just knew they'd lost. That afternoon proved to me the Barmy Army in full voice would always get to the Aussies and rattle them. Broady and I put on 87 for the eighth wicket. *Wisden* would later say the stand 'might have been the most important of the series'. We secured a lead of 145, which meant that we took the momentum into our bowling in the second innings and then Steven Finn did his magic. He had come in because Woody was injured, and had not played for two years; now he grabbed six wickets. But with the lower Australian order showing resistance I was called upon to bowl and got the final wicket of Starc. The total of 121 required to win was never going to be a problem and we wrapped it up in three days. And being 2-1 up with two Tests to play we were now in a great position for Trent Bridge.

The drama for that Test began even before the toss took place. It was clear if we won the toss we had to put them in. Cooky was firmly of that opinion and so were the rest of us. All except Broady. This is Broady's home ground. In such a situation the home town player is supposed to know what you should do. He wanted to bat first. I couldn't believe what he was saying but then I remembered Broady is always dead against bowling first. Even at Edgbaston Broady wanted us to bat. He always wanted to bat first even if it was a green wicket and was overcast. Broady would say, 'No, no, we're going to have to bat first.' Broady is not alone in this. Bowlers often react like that. Maybe they feel a pressure when asked to bowl first. After all if you bowl first you have to try and bowl the opposition out. I am sure opening bowlers get a bit nervous about that. I have seen it happen in club cricket. There is always a guy who insists on batting no matter what. But it isn't only opening bowlers who get nervous. Murali was the most nervous of bowlers. When in a Test Sri Lanka were thinking of declaring he would say, 'No, let's get another 100.' But Cooky was not going to listen to

Broady and said, 'We're going to bowl if we win the toss.' And win it we did.

What followed was magic. Broady didn't want to bowl but with Jimmy not playing Cooky threw him the ball at the start of the innings and 9.3 overs later he was walking off the field having taken 8 for 15, with only Warner and their wicketkeeper Peter Nevill not falling to him. That is the best spell of bowling I have seen, the best session of cricket I've ever had in my life. Absolutely amazing. It was the best feeling I have had on a cricket field. In an hour and a half we had bowled Australia out for 60 in 18.3 overs. As Broady was destroying the Australians, I kept telling myself, 'I just can't believe this is happening.' We came back into the dressing room before lunch and I was pinching myself. The heavy roller was on and we had bowled the Aussies out for 60.

Then Rooty scored a century, 130, and on the second day Broady and I did what we had been doing right through the series. We played some shots putting on 58 for the ninth wicket. We had a huge lead of 331 and this time Stokesy got in on the act with a career-best 6 for 36 – and we had won back the Ashes by the morning of the third day, winning by an innings and 78 runs.

We did lose the Oval Test. It was a really flat wicket and maybe we relaxed a bit mentally. After we had celebrated the series win with the urn the Australians, having refused to talk to or even acknowledge us for the entire series, came over to our changing room and had a chat. That is when I actually spoke to the player who'd called me Osama for the first time since that brief exchange on the Cardiff pitch. He came up to me and said, 'I know what you thought I said, but I didn't say that. I've got Muslim friends and some of my best friends are Muslims.'

I did not argue with him. But I was so clear that is what he said. Why should I invent it out of the blue? I've got nothing against him. I have never had any fights with him before. I did not even know the guy. And I thought his denial was a standard response.

However, as the Australians left our changing room and we celebrated winning the Ashes, I was able to forget the Osama comment. There was so much to enjoy, winning the Ashes in front of my family, my wife and my in-laws who live in London. I walked on the pitch with my son later that summer evening when the light in this country is so soft and magical, and then as the lads started singing and drinking I knew it was time to go home.

I was no Osama. I never had been. My England teammates did not think so. They knew I was a devout Muslim. They respected that but didn't find it in any way strange or weird. What is more, neither did the English fans. The beard was no longer something to be mocked or abused but accepted – as much a part of English cricket culture as W. G. Grace's beard had been. My faith may be different but I was as English as the rest of the team. If after the Cardiff game I had felt I was now an England player, at the Oval, holding the urn in my hand and bringing the Ashes back home was for me the defining summer of my career. Having waited so long to get the England call, and even thinking that I might never get it, I had finally arrived. Nobody could question that or take that away from me.

CHAPTER 12

THE BEARD GOES ABROAD

Growing up I would meet older cricketers, many of them from Pakistan, and listen to their stories – told to me in some sorrow – about the impossibility of getting England to tour Pakistan, or at least send a full-strength side to that country when they were young. They had to rely on so-called Commonwealth teams, some of them put together by the former England and Lancashire wicketkeeper George Duckworth. But here I was in October 2015, exactly a month after I had left the sunlit Oval with my wife and son, playing Pakistan and there was no question this was England's best side. Except, given world events, we were playing Pakistan not at home but in Abu Dhabi, as due to the security situation they had not played a home Test since 2009. And I had a new responsibility. I was now opening the Test batting, Cooky's seventh opening partner since Straussy had retired in 2012. It allowed the team to fit in two spinners and was thought to balance the side. But I found this quite hard because I was bowling 30 to 40 overs and then having to open the batting straightaway. I found that it affected my batting quite a bit and while I had opened regularly in white-ball cricket I had opened in a four-day match for Worcester only once. It takes a bit of adjustment. The heat did not help. The temperature was around 45 degrees and we were using ice towels and drinking rehydration fluids to replace salt and minerals.

In the first Test I walked out with Cooky to open after bowling 30 overs, only four less than Rash. Cooky, who went on to make 263, would later say he was in 'a blissful state' during that innings. I cannot claim to have been in that state of mind but we put on 116, our best opening stand of the series, of which I made 35. This was the first time I had batted with Cooky in a Test and it was very different to batting with Broady or Bluey Bairstow. Cooky does not say much in the middle. Normally in a partnership when you come together in the middle at the end of the over or after one of you has hit a four, you talk to your partner not only about the cricket but what's going on at the ground, indeed everything and anything. It varies. You often talk just to take the pressure off. But during this stand I did not have the chats with Cooky that I'd had with Broady during our Ashes partnerships. Or the ones I have since had with Bluey. Then we would often come into the middle between overs and say, 'Look at that guy in the crowd, look what he's doing.' Once with Bluey I hit one into the changing room and Bluey came up to see and said, 'What's that guy doing there, I think he just wants to get on the camera.' To be fair, during that stand with Cooky neither of us could have pointed to the crowd because despite the fact that there was a large Pakistani population in the UAE there was hardly anyone watching, so all we could have pointed to were empty rows of seats. Indeed, *lack* of crowds held play up on the last afternoon: when Bluey, going for runs as we chased victory, hit Wahab Riaz for a six over deep midwicket, the fact that the stands were empty meant it took some time to get the ball back. Had there been people sitting there the ball would have been tossed back immediately. The local Pakistanis did come out for the one-day matches, once again underlining how subcontinental crowds no longer care for Test cricket. To perform well in the UAE you have to change your style of play. I had to take my time and try to grind the opposition down.

Although the wicket for the first Test was slow and did not help spin, we bowled Pakistan out for 173 in the second innings, Rash got five and I got a couple including bowling their captain Misbah-ul-Haq. We nearly won the first game. We needed 99 to win from at best nineteen overs. But it was never likely that number would be bowled. We had to score from almost every ball – I got out doing so and so did Stokesy, Bluey Bairstow and Jos Buttler – but in the end it got dark and we just couldn't do it. Then we lost the next two Tests, playing poorly. My bowling was okay but Rash and I came under a great deal of pressure because we were spinners and in Asia spinners are expected to take wickets. Some of the wickets turned. But when it turned it was towards the end of the Test and none of the three venues, Abu Dhabi, Dubai and Sharjah, were like the great spinning wickets that we expect in Asia. Who knows what would have happened had we won in Abu Dhabi? Pakistan celebrated that escape by winning the next two Tests, in which I bowled a total of 70 overs. I felt drained at the end of the series.

I also had to cope with the drama of receiving a call in the middle of the Dubai Test which shook me. Dad had been taken to the local hospital and was close to dying. I was playing in a floodlit warm-up match in Abu Dhabi before the T20 which was due to be held in Dubai three days later. Dad had flown into Dubai to watch me play. Dad takes up the story:

We had decided to do some shopping on that day, because the following day we had arranged with Moeen to go out on a boat. So, that particular day we went to this place where all the Asians are and there is Pakistani and Indian style of food and clothing. My wife wanted to get a few things. We had to cross a little river to get there and at seven o'clock a driver came to pick us up, but his car was parked on the other side of the river and we had to catch a boat to cross this river to get to the car. I was happy. We had done our shopping. I'd had some lovely biryani. But as I tried to step onto the boat somehow I missed my footing and I went into the sea. I can't remember anything else. I was told later I fell into the sea unconscious. I hit my head on the floor and they said that according to the medical records for 35 seconds I was completely dead. Normally I wear trousers and a shirt but because I went to the Pakistani and Indian areas I was wearing a Shalwar kameez and as I fell in the water, the water must have got into my Shalwar kameez and floated me up. You could say my Shalwar kameez saved me. My wife saw me floating and she and the driver pulled me out. I can remember vomiting the water out. They sat me down and bent me forward and the water just gushed out of me. There must have been a couple of feet of water that came out of my mouth. Everything was going round and round in my head and I know that a lot of people had gathered. Maybe the doctor or paramedic was there. Then a policeman came and said, 'Did anybody push you?' I could hardly talk. The water was gushing out of my mouth and I shook my head a little bit and I said no. He went away. The next thing I knew I was in the ambulance and I went to the hospital. I was semiconscious and they put a big mask on my face because I wasn't breathing properly. Then they put this heart machine on and they asked me a few questions. My wife had to provide all the answers and told them I was diabetic and all the details of my medical condition. The problem now was we had to get in touch with Moeen and everybody else in the family. My phone had dropped into the sea where I fell. And my wife couldn't get hold of Moeen because he was playing at the time in the warm-up match and his phone was off. So she rang Firuza in Birmingham and Firuza contacted the ECB.

That is when I was told what had happened to Dad and, accompanied by the England doctor, I rushed to the hospital. This must have been around one o'clock in the morning. I had come after visiting hours but with the England doctor by my side they allowed me to see Dad. I saw Dad under a mask and he later told me that he saw my shadow from under his mask. I held his hand and seeing the mask and all those machines and needles in Dad I got frightened. I would have wanted to stay with him but they would only allow me to stay for a minute or so. Dad was in intensive care for about four or five days and Kadeer, Azba and Chacha Shabir flew in. I went every day to see him and so did the England doctor. Dad was later to tell me how on the plane back to England as he dozed off he had a vision of falling in the sea. I found it hard to concentrate on the matches.

I played in only two of the three T20 games, failing to score in either, but was economical with my bowling and got a wicket in each match. We won all three with the last match ending with an incredible over where Chris bowled superbly, all six balls being yorkers which meant Pakistan scored only three and Morgy and Jos saw us home. We had also won the 50-over white-ball inter-nationals and this showed the improvement we had made since the World Cup. We came away from the UAE with something to be happy about: that for all our failings in red-ball cricket, we could win away from home in the white-ball formats.

The Pakistan series was also one where the bonds between Rash and me got stronger. Rash is one of my best friends in cricket. We have known each other since the age of twelve. He was so good he was playing in the year above me. The first time I met him was when we played in the regional festivals against each other, Midlands against the North and the South. We played in the Lions together. After that we used to spend time together; both of our families are from Kashmir and we speak the language. I got to know his family quite well too and we get on really well both personally and on a family level. He is of a Muslim background and very devout, he does his prayers and we talk about Allah. We speak pretty much every other day. Rash is very entertaining. Once we were talking in the dressing room about who is smarter, me or him. We always talk about things like that. I said to him, in front of everyone, what's a tangerine? I asked him that question because I knew he would not know what a tangerine was. However, his reaction surprised me. He started to jump up and down and I was thinking why is he jumping up and down? Does he think it is a monkey? Then he said a tangerine is what you jump on. I realized that he thought a tangerine was a trampoline. We all burst into laughter and to Rash's credit he joined in as well. He can take a joke.

He is the most skilful leg-spinner out there. I've not seen a leg-spinner with more talent than him. In the ODIs and T20s he's always taking wickets and I feel we have built up a great partnership in white-ball cricket. At one end I try and bowl as tight as I can and build some pressure for him and he can attack and often ends up taking a lot of wickets. It hasn't quite worked out in Test matches but given time I am sure it would.

On this tour to the UAE we spent our days and evenings together, we did everything together. If we all decided we were going for dinner, Rash and I came as a pair. If anyone was inviting me, then basically they were inviting Adil as well, that's how tight we are. Some of the guys did take the mickey out of us for being so close. That did worry me a bit. You don't want to make out that it's an ethnic thing or that we are a clique in the team or anything of that kind. I was reassured by Trevor Bayliss in Dubai that it was nothing to be worried about. He came up to me one day and he said it's fantastic that you are both together and good friends, and both being spinners you can talk. He basically said don't change from now on. If anything, he said, Rash and you should mingle in a bit more. I was so happy he said that because I didn't want anybody to think we were always together because we were Asians, as it wasn't like that. Our friendship was based on the fact that we had known each other for such a long time, shared so many things and, despite being spinners and in theory in competition with each other, did not feel we had to keep ourselves apart.

A month after the last T20 in Sharjah we were playing our first Test in South Africa, a series all the experts thought we could not possibly win. But in the first and only warm-up match at Pietermaritzburg I took 6 for 77 in the second innings – my first six-wicket haul for England since the one against India at the Rose Bowl – and we won by an innings and 91 runs. And this was not a nothing South African A side. Two guys had played Test cricket, and we were to meet four more during the series ahead.

My good form with the ball continued in the first Test at Durban. In the first innings Broady demolished the top order, I got the other half of their batting, taking 4 for 69, and was very pleased with the way, just before the end of the second day's play, I got Faf du Plessis to charge at me and bowled him.

We set South Africa 416 to win and on the final morning with South Africa 136 for 4 and de Villiers 37 not out, a draw was not impossible. I had at that stage not yet taken a wicket. Cooky asked me to open the bowling and I decided to bowl round the wicket to de Villiers. I pitched it on leg, de Villiers stayed back, the ball stayed low and Aleem Dar put his finger up for lbw. De Villiers reviewed but I was confident and the review showed the ball had just grazed the leg-stump. Umpire's call. I would have hated it had he given it not out, but now I could not be happier. I also had Bavuma and Abbott, whom I had also got in the first innings, and the interesting thing about getting Bavuma out was Bluey stumped him, England's first Test stumping for three years. Every spinner likes nothing better than getting the batsman to charge down the track, deceiving him in flight and have the wicketkeeper behind the stumps do the rest. That is when as a bowler you feel you are a magician, able to bamboozle the audience about what you are doing. That morning South Africa lost their last six wickets for 38, and I finished with 3 for 47 and the Man of the Match award.

I travelled to Cape Town for the second Test in great heart. I have spent a lot of time in Cape Town, playing a couple of times for the local club, St Augustine's. I bowled one more over, 52 as opposed to 51 at Durban but at Cape Town I did not get a wicket. But this will remain for me one of the most amazing games of cricket I have ever played in. The match saw four hundreds, two each by an Englishman and a South African, and the first century by a black South African player after 127 years of Test cricket. That was by Temba Bavuma. His innings came on the fourth day and, epoch-making as it was, it had been preceded by the best innings I've ever seen. It was played by an Englishman, Ben Stokes. He had come in on a hat-trick on the first evening when, after winning the toss and making a good start, we lost Nick Compton and James Taylor to successive balls, bowled by Kagiso Rabada either side of tea. Then Stokesy produced batting that was quite astonishing. The South African pace bowlers were quick but Stokesy was on a different level during that innings. Watching it from the sidelines it was hard to believe. He and Bluey put on 399 for the sixth wicket, the highest for that wicket ever in Test history. Had they made 12 more they would have had the highest for any wicket. But it was not so much the stats as the way Stokesy treated the bowling. Bluey helped of course and watching them bat was like seeing wave after wave pound the South Africans. Just when their bowlers thought the tide had receded on would come another wave and wash everything away. But wonderful as this was to see I must say for me it was very hard. I could not relax.

The reason was I was in next. I was padded up because if we lost a wicket I was going to have to go in quickly. I tried to keep myself busy. During their stand I must have had five or six snoozes all with my pads on. But you've got to watch for a bit and while you are doing that you are squinting and concentrating. You cannot watch every ball during such a long partnership. You go off and try and do something, but your mind is still on the game. Then there comes a point where you think, right, they are in now, just forget about the cricket for a bit. They're safe; they're not getting out soon. So you can relax. That is the dangerous bit. And to cap it all there is Cooky saying you cannot move from your position because if you do you will disturb the hold Stokes and Bairstow have got on the South Africans and one of them will get out. That is Cooky's superstition, and he insists you respect it.

Stokesy was finally out on the second afternoon. Having hit a six for his 250, he hit another six and then got out. At last I gathered up my gloves and bat and walked out to the wicket. With the score 622 for 6 and Bluey on 146, as I left Cooky said, 'We're going to pull out. We'll let him get his 150.' Stokesy had got out at the end of the over, so Bluey was to face the next ball and as I arrived at the middle I just went up to Bluey and told him what Cooky had said and then added, 'Get to your hundred and fifty this over. I do not want to face a ball.' The thought that he might not get to 150 that over and I would then have to take the bowling did not fill me with pleasure. We had got to where we wanted to be. Bluey understood. The second ball of that over he pulled for six and I was relieved. I did not face a ball, thank God. What made this moment special is that I had been in that situation in club cricket. That is something you get used to in that level of the game. I'd walk in and say, 'Bro, you know what, get your fifty, I don't even want to face a ball, just get your fifty and we walk off.' But in a Test series you don't see that. That day a Test match at Newlands was transformed into the cricket I played at Moseley in my youth.

I bowled as well as I had at the Wanderers, but good bowling does not always get its reward. Hashim Amla, without lighting up the sky as Stokesy had done, responded with a double century of his own. It was then that the Barmy Army responded to the South African crowd and made me feel very special, showing how much society both in South Africa and England has changed.

As Amla batted the Cape Town crowd sang what they call the Kolo Touré song. The South African crowd in one part of Newlands would rise and sing, 'Hashim, Hashim, Hashim, Hashim Amla' and sit down. Then the Barmy Army, which was in another part, would get up and sing 'Moeen, Moeen, Moeen Ali' and sit down. I reckon this went on for hours and both Hashim and I would smile and wave to the crowd. When I was born that would have been unimaginable. Nelson Mandela was in prison in Robben Island, which you can see from Cape Town's Table Mountain, and South Africa was ruled by a regime which said non-whites were subhuman. To listen to that song in such a city and having been to a school which bore Mandela's name was unbelievably moving. What is more the two cricketers the crowds were honouring were both Muslims with beards and one of them, Amla, had been called a terrorist on air by Dean Jones, the former Australian cricketer. The Barmy Army would have been mostly white as well. I don't think a lot of Asian people are in the Barmy Army, not for racist reasons, but because not many of them could afford to see a Test series in South Africa, not just for the cost of flights and accommodation, but also the time off work. And most of the South Africans that day in Newlands were also white, showing how far this country so long in the grip of apartheid has come.

This was made all the sweeter when A. B. de Villiers came up to me after the series and said, 'I'm going to tell you something, I sing the song to my son and it's the only thing my son goes quiet about. That's the song my son sings most of the time. So when my son is playing cricket, he says, "I'll be Hashim Amla, you be Moeen Ali", or he'll be Moeen Ali, I'll be Hashim Amla. And we both sing.' What could better demonstrate sport's and cricket's power to bridge cultures and races: South Africa's best batsman, a white Afrikaner, singing the name of England's Muslim cricketer with his son.

As it happened Amla gave up the captaincy after the Cape Town Test. De Villiers took over but nothing the South Africans did could stop Broady at the Wanderers. On the third day with both innings completed we were just 10 ahead but batting second. At lunch South Africa were 16 without loss and Trevor gave us a talking-to or, as Cooky put it, 'a kick up the arse'. When we went back out, Broady saw himself back at Trent Bridge against Australia and in 12.1 overs blew South Africa away, taking 6 for 17. Jimmy and Finny gave him good support, and our close catching was brilliant. South Africa made 83 and we had won the Test and the series long before the end of the third day's play. I had my best score with the bat in the first innings of the fourth Test at Centurion, making 61 and really timing the ball sweetly, but overall our effort fell below the standards we had set in the first three. Rabada did a sort of Broady, taking 6 for 32 in our second innings, we made 101 in our second and lost by 280 runs. Yes, we had once again lost the last Test of a series but to win 2-1 away from home in an age when teams win at home and lose away, and that in South Africa where few teams win, showed that our Test cricket after the defeats against Pakistan was coming good.

If the defeat at Centurion was deflating what happened immediately after the Test match was uplifting and made you realize the value of sport. Unlike Australia in the summer as I have mentioned, after the match the South Africans would be welcoming and invite us to their dressing room. Now after Centurion they invited us over into their changing room for their end-of-series fines meeting. I've been to a few fines meetings and the Proteas' one was the best by a mile. Morne Morkel was running it and it involved players from each side pairing up in the middle of the room, making jokes about things that had happened during the series. It was very funny.

I like to play cricket as hard I can and I also have friends from the opposing teams who I can talk to, go out for meals with in the evenings, and then the next day I'm bowling against them, trying to get them out. When we socialize in the evening we won't really talk about the cricket. It's more talking about how things are going, our families and things like that. The South Africans reminded us that is what cricket should be about. With bat and ball you will do everything to win. Once the contest is over you will remember you are men given the chance of playing a game which provides you with a very good living and that can bring joy and fun to a lot of people. Not many people can say that of their lives.

CHAPTER 13

ALL THE ASIANS

n one of those quirks of fixture planning in cricket, between May and December 2016 I played against all the four Asian Test nations, starting with Sri Lanka, the country I had made my debut against, and ending with a Test in India. Sandwiched between the two was a home series against Pakistan and my first visit as an England Test player to Bangladesh.

I had begun the summer well. In one of the rare opportunities an England contracted player gets to play for his county I played three matches for Worcestershire all before the middle of May, and the second of them was against Gloucestershire at Bristol. With the first Sri Lanka Test only three weeks away, it was comforting to see my batting was in the right groove. You can practise as much as you like in the nets but unless you play a competitive match you never know how good your form is. In Bristol that chilly, late-April day I made 74 in the first innings, helping us to a small but handy lead and then with Gloucester setting us 352 to win in 63 overs, I knew we had a challenge on our hands. They were keen. They had not won at Bristol for two years and I came in with the score 10 for 1 and we were soon 49 for 3. Liam Norwell, their right-arm fast-medium bowler, was proving a handful. In such situations defence is useless and while we kept losing wickets, I made 136 from 144 balls and made sure we did not lose.

As sportsmen we always say what matters is the match we are playing not past history, but as I journeyed to Leeds for the first Test against Sri Lanka I did think of the past. After all it was only two years earlier and on that very ground that I had scored my maiden hundred for England in my second Test and only just failed to prevent the Sri Lankans from winning. However, this time I was confident that we would not be in a similar position and right enough Bluey with the bat and Jimmy with the ball made sure there was no such drama. On his home ground, and with his mother who works there watching, Bluey hit 140 and then Jimmy took a five-fer in both innings to ensure we didn't have to bat again. Having been out for a duck in our innings, my only contribution came with the ball in their second innings: I bowled just one over, gave away two runs but bowled Dinesh Chandimal, their number four, for 8.

They say you need luck in this game. Yes, I did have luck in the second Test at Chester-le-Street. I came in to bat on the first evening after Cooky had won the toss. I had 28 by the close with Woakesy partnering me on 8. I was well aware that 310 for 6 on the first day meant if I did not make sure the lower order made runs we would not have a winning score. This is where luck came in. I had got to 36 the next morning when I edged Nuwan Pradeep and the ball somehow went through Dimuth Karunaratne's hands at second slip. Woakesy was also dropped in the next over and I knew what we had to do. I could trust Woakes to keep ticking away while I tried to make sure that anything hittable was despatched. The Sri Lankans thought Herath, their most experienced bowler, would test me. I had decided I would not let the left-arm spinner settle into his bowling rhythm. He needed one wicket to reach 300, a landmark only Murali and Chaminda Vaas have achieved for the Sri Lankans, and that sort of thing can prey on your mind despite what players say. I wanted to make sure Herath didn't know what length he could bowl to me; at times I would come forward, at other times I went back. The Sri Lankans did play into my hands. After Woakesy had gone for 39 – we had put on 92 for the seventh wicket – for once Broady and I didn't have our customary late-order partnership. Then the Sri Lankans decided that Finny could not bat. This is despite the fact that he had scored a Test-saving 50 against New Zealand. But when he was on strike the Sri Lankans put close catchers around him. Perhaps Herath thought this was the easiest chance to get to 300 wickets. Meanwhile I was left vast spaces to explore. Often, even with two balls of the over left, the field did not come in and I could choose when to pick up the single to retain the strike. After 70 minutes of this the Sri Lankan strategy of 'get Finny' finally worked and Herath got his 300th wicket when Finny was caught and bowled for 10. But by then we had put on 72, our score was 498, I was 155 not out, and Cooky could declare.

Then, after Jimmy, Broady and Woakesy had bundled out Sri Lanka for 101, Cooky made history of sorts when in a move now rarely seen in Test cricket he decided to enforce the follow-on. There was more resistance in the second innings. Having bowled only 4 overs in the first, I bowled 28 overs, getting the wicket of Thirimanne. Victory was never in doubt. It would have been great to complete a 3-0 sweep at Lord's but rain made sure there could not be a result.

But despite having scored a hundred and laid the foundation for our innings victory, as we came to Lord's for the first Test against Pakistan it was back to the old media chorus of 'should Moeen be in the team'? This time it was not my batting but my bowling that was given as the reason why I should be dropped. I actually bowled quite well and in the second innings, got two of Pakistan's main batsmen, Younis Khan and captain Misbah-ul-Haq, the latter for 0, helping bowl out Pakistan for 215 which meant we had a final-day target of 283. Then I was out to a bad shot and it was now Moeen the batsman under the microscope. There is no denying my dismissal in the second innings was embarrassing. We were playing for a draw and with the fourth ball I faced from their leg-spinner Yasir Shah I danced down the wicket and had a massive hoik and was bowled for 2. Yasir Shah is not a great spinner of the ball, and the ball that got me was straight. I just missed it.

As I returned to the dressing room I started joking about my shot with Farby and a few of the lads and they were surprised that I could joke about the shot I had played. I had felt really embarrassed by my shot as I walked back to the pavilion. But I saw it as just one of those things, that was my game and I couldn't get too down about it. You have to take such things in your stride and not make it look like one bad shot is the end of the world. We lost the game and once again the media was on my back. I was supposed to have lost my wits when I played that shot against Yasir Shah. I hadn't. I had the right idea but executed it badly. There is a difference between not knowing what you are doing and trying to do something you know is right but failing to pull it off.

But as the next Test at Old Trafford showed the English fans did not share this media hostility. There was a huge roar of 'The Beard that's feared' when, on the second afternoon, I came out to join Bluey after Rooty had got out for a quite magnificent 254. Bluey was on the brink of his 50. But, unlike Cape Town, I didn't have to tell him that I didn't want to face a ball. He had a bit of time and I did face a few, making 2. The moment Bluey got to his 50, Cooky – who'd made a fine century on the first day – declared at 589. I got a chance to bowl, 7 overs and four balls, breaking the ninth-wicket stand of 60 between Misbah-ul-Haq and their number ten, Wahab Riaz, which was proving very irritating, first getting Misbah, their top scorer, and then Riaz to wrap up the innings. Pakistan's target was 565 to win, or more realistically bat for eleven hours for the draw, and this time I had much more bowling to do, more than all our other bowlers. I got their opener Mohammad Hafeez, then Younis again, making sure his miserable series continued, and as in the first innings I ended their innings and the match when to my great satisfaction I had Yasir lbw. A victory by 330 runs could not have been more emphatic and showed that, disappointing as Lord's was, we could bounce back.

Though I had not batted well at Lord's and wasn't required to do anything with the bat at Old Trafford, I came back to my home ground at Edgbaston confident I could score. I must say I was a bit surprised when Misbah decided to put us in but in his previous nine Tests he had never lost when he inserted the opposition and his decision seemed dead right when in mid-afternoon I walked out to the middle with the score 158 for 5, Cooky, Hales, Rooty, Vincey and Bluey all gone. I now had to bat as if I was Worcester's number three, not England's number seven.

Gazza was batting well and he and I put on 68. After he left I curbed my natural instincts to take the attack to the opposition to make sure we got near to 300, but we fell three short. Pakistan's batsmen made us realize it was not nearly enough as they got to 400. To make matters worse our second innings was one of those efforts where we seemed secure and then suddenly were facing the abyss. When I joined Bluey on the fourth afternoon we had lost half our side and were just 179 ahead, hardly a position of comfort. Pakistan could dream.

That is when Bluey and I had our best stand for England. By the close we had put on 122, taking England to 414 for 5. Yasir Shah bowled the first over on the final day and I had no fears of repeating my embarrassing error from Lord's. This time I scored 19 off him in that opening over. Even if you start with the best of intentions, failure can make you look so stupid while success forgives everything you do, however outlandish your plans. I was 86 not out when Cooky declared on 445 for 6. It would have been nice to score a hundred on ground where I learnt my cricket but the team must always come first.

We needed to bowl Pakistan out quickly as Cooky had given us 84 overs to win the match. We had no fear that they would be able to score the 343 they needed to win. In the end we required 70.5 overs with that final ball of the Pakistani innings bowled by me. I had earlier had Azhar Ali. He had made 139 in the first innings and played the central role in giving Pakistan a lead of 103. This time he made 38 and I broke the second-wicket stand, which had added 73 and looked like it might thwart us. Then with an hour and a half to go, their last-wicket pair was frustrating us and Cooky brought me on again. That is when with the fifth ball of my seventeenth over I caught and bowled their number ten Sohail Khan, who had made 36. Now the celebrations could begin. What felt really nice was that I was again part of winning that game and making a contribution. And this was such a team effort. In one of those rare symmetries all our bowlers, Jimmy, Broady, Woaksy, Finny and I got two wickets each, something the statisticians later said had not happened for an England side for 35 years. (Only Rooty missed out but then he bowled just one over.) From one down we were 2-1 ahead and Lord's seemed a distant memory.

We went to the Oval confident we could wrap up the series, but after winning the toss we again made a bad start and I walked in mid-afternoon with the score 110 for 5, with Cooky, Baz, Rooty, Vincey and Gazza all out. Wahab was on fire, he had three of the five wickets and the Pakistanis had clearly read all the media about me not being able to deal with the short ball. The first ball Wahab bowled hit me on the helmet with such force that the ball rebounded to backward point. Wahab may have thought after that I would take fright. I watched the next two balls carefully, then the third one I flicked to square-leg for four. With Bluey, as he can do at his best, wielding his white-rose broadsword, I decided the rapier would be the best tactic for dealing with this Pakistani attack. The cricket writer Osman Samiuddin would later see this innings as 'a demonstration of liquid exquisiteness of sporting movement more commonly associated with Roger Federer – whips here, lashes there, the entire operation orchestrated by soft and powerful wrists. It was the best of his three Test hundreds.' By the time I was last out for 108 we had made 328, not awesome but more than looked likely when I came in and a total we felt we could defend.

Younis Khan had struggled all summer, a once great cricketer who seemed to be playing one series too many, but now suddenly he rediscovered himself. He was helped not only by the Pakistani coaches but also by a telephone call from Mohammad Azharuddin in India. Younis scored 218, we did not bowl well and they took a first innings lead of 214. I had some consolation in getting Wahab's wicket, luring him forward while Bluey whipped his bails off.

When Bluey and I came together at 128 for 5, still 86 behind, I felt we might repeat our Edgbaston rescue but after we had added 65, I fell for 32 and our score of 253 meant Pakistan had only 40 to make, which they did without losing a wicket. It meant a lot to the Pakistanis to win at the Oval where they had triumphed on their first visit back in 1954 and just as one of their great batsmen Hanif Mohammad, who played in that first Oval Test, was dying. For us it raised the much-debated question, to which I have no answer: why do we come to the Oval for the last Test, either having won a series or being ahead, but then go on to lose?

But while the fact that we had failed to win the series was hard to take, I had every reason to feel happy with my game. In the England batting averages, I was second to Rooty, the unquestioned leader, with 316 runs at an average 63.20, and my 11 wickets were more than twice Finny's and two ahead of Jimmy. And off the field the series could not have gone better. England–Pakistan series in the past have often been marked by dreadful strife, notably a Test at the Oval in a previous series won by England on account of Pakistan forfeiting a match for the first time in history after their players were accused of ball-tampering. This series had been played in the best of spirits. A photograph summed it up. It showed Cooky, his arm round Misbah-ul-Haq's shoulder, escorting him off the Oval at the end of the series. The sign read Investec Test Series Drawn 2016 and in the background stood the trophy neither of us had been able to claim. What the cameras did not catch was the Pakistani players asking me to lead them in prayers. That meant a lot to me.

I knew there was more Asian cricket for us but three months before we headed for Bangladesh there was a terrorist attack on an upmarket café in Dhaka killing twenty-four people including some Westerners. Five militants were killed in the army's response. Immediately there were questions as to whether it was safe to go there. The ECB carried out a security review before we flew out. Morgy decided not to go and at the end of day that was an individual decision that you have to respect. There was no question of me ducking out of the tour. Bangladesh is where my wife's family come from. I had been there, played cricket and knew how much their public loved the game. This was once a football country but in recent years it has taken to cricket and I have always felt we should do all we can to encourage the game there. Australia had decided not to tour Bangladesh in 2015 and four months after our tour, when the Under-19 World Cup took place, they did not send a team. Many in Bangladesh feared that, like Pakistan, they would have to wander the world to find a place to play. I felt England should do everything to prevent that. Certainly we could not complain about the security. In Dhaka a 2,000-strong security team followed our coach from the hotel to the ground. The ground itself was ringed with security with a one-kilometre blockade round it and CCTV covered the stadium. The security was the best I had ever seen and I felt another country would do well to make us any safer. The Bangladesh crowd appreciated the fact that we had toured with banners held up at grounds saying 'Thank U England'.

Interestingly, the only time the security was breached was just before our opening one-day warm up at Fatullah when three old ladies in a tuk-tuk somehow managed to slip into the convoy that was carrying us to the ground. We had a good laugh over that and it certainly did not affect our play. We won that match by four wickets, I scored 70 and Jos Buttler who was skippering the side made 80. Our preparation continued to go well as we won the ODI series 2-1.

Bangladesh, never having beaten England at Test level, were desperate to do so and made no secret that they had prepared wickets that would last three or at most four days and would turn and make life difficult for our batters. Having for most of my England career been the only spinner I suddenly found myself in the first Test at Chittagong as one of three spinners along with Gareth Batty (who'd been recalled after a seven-year absence) and Rash. Chittagong was drier than we expected but it turned from the first ball. I also had a new batting position, not as high as number three for Worcester, but number five, and walked out to join Rooty with the score at 21 for 3. I had decided I would cover my off-stump and sweep whenever I could. It left me open to lbw and Bangladesh, in particular Shakib Al Hasan, appealed often. Five times Bangladesh thought they had me out leg-before, three of the reviews coming in six balls from Shakib either side of lunch, but I survived them all. Rooty was a brilliant adviser: twice in one over after lunch he persuaded me I should appeal and his judgement was perfect. After he was out, followed by Stokesy, I revived my summer rescue act with

Bluey. We converted 106 for 5 to 194 when I was out for 68, which was the highest score of the innings.

Batting first for 292 may not have seemed a great outcome but in a low-scoring Test it proved the highest score of the match. Cooky opened with the spin of Gareth Batty, then brought Rash on before turning to me, but I ended up bowling more than anyone else. With the Chittagong wicket being so dry, I decided I would bowl faster than I normally bowl and chose to go round the wicket to get both turn and drift against the three Bangladeshi left-handers in their top order. While Tamim Iqbal resisted I took the wickets of two of the left-handers, got Shakib as well and then with Stokesy causing the tail to collapse we got a handy lead. Stokesy's batting also made the difference to our second innings, which left Bangladesh needing 286 to win. Many felt Cooky had been wrong to select three spinners but I got Tamim when he had only scored 9, and had Shakib caught behind as well. Batty pitched in with three and Rash got another one, and between us we got all the top six in their order. While the winning margin was tight we were always confident.

We arrived in Mirpur for the second Test expecting another spinning wicket to find one that, while it was a turner, was much darker and damper. Surrey's Zafar Ansari, making his Test debut, had replaced Batty as the third spinner. This time Cooky turned to me first when he brought on spin. Tamim Iqbal, Bangladesh's best batsman, had played beautifully, driving me and the other bowlers fluently. He and Mominul Haque had put on 170 for the second wicket when he padded up to me and I trapped him lbw. This triggered an amazing collapse where they lost their last nine wickets for 49 runs. I picked up four more, bowling Mominul and getting the wickets of captain Mushfiqur Rahim, Mehidy Hasan and Kamrul Islam. It was my second five-fer and I must say I had a bit of luck. As I admitted afterwards to the press, 'I'm nowhere near where I want to be as a spinner. I don't really have much success.' I have always believed that you should face facts, whatever they are.

We should have done better with the bat. I made only 10 as we managed a lead of only 24. Then when we bowled in their second innings we should have been more positive with the use of DRS, the decision-review system that allows players and on-field umpires to ask for the third umpire to review decisions using TV replays and other electronic sensors. On two occasions I was convinced the batsman was out lbw but we decided not to review when if we had, DRS would have proved me right. We were left 272 to chase and while it was 64 more than we had ever successfully chased in Asia, Cooky and Ben Duckett, his latest opening partner, took us to 100 by tea on the third day in only 23 overs. But after tea we collapsed, I was lbw to Mehidy without scoring and ten wickets fell for 64 runs. Bangladesh had finally beaten us in a Test match. You could see from their joy what it meant to defeat England. Sad as it was to lose the Test I agreed with their captain Mushfiqur that the ICC needed to send 'the big boys' of cricket to play Bangladesh. Cooky was right when he very generously said that it was a good win for Bangladesh and would help develop their cricket.

The Mirpur defeat meant we came to India as underdogs, which we did not mind. India were ranked number one in the world having won twelve of their previous thirteen home Tests. The only one they failed to win was rain affected. We had beaten India in 2012, which Cooky saw as one of the great triumphs of his career. This, of course, was a new Indian cricket world. After nearly a quarter of a century there was no Sachin Tendulkar; I never did get a chance to play against him. We were now in the world of what the Indians called the Kohli effect, since Kohli had taken over the captaincy from M. S. Dhoni. Virat Kohli comes across on TV as aggressive and always wanting to get in a fight. While India was fielding he would gesture to the crowd to get behind the team almost in the style of a football player and in this series he certainly tried to rile Stokesy. There was a dramatic moment in Mohali in the third Test when, after Ashwin had successfully reviewed a lbw decision against Stokesy, Kohli put his fingers to his lips, looking like a schoolmaster and apparently trying to calm things down when it actually stirred them up. However, I had played cricket with him in my Under-19 days and spent a bit of time with him. Off the field I knew he was a very nice, friendly guy with whom I never had any problems. The public perception of a human being and the reality can often be different and Kohli illustrates that perfectly.

The hard public face of Kohli emerged in the first Test but it was directed not at us but the groundsman at Rajkot, a new stadium, where the first Test was being played. The pitch of black cotton soil was livelier than Kohli wanted, it had some live grass but despite the cracks did not disintegrate as Indian pitches can, and after the match Kohli told the groundsman off, saying, 'That should not have been the case.' Kohli might have been even more annoyed had we won at Rajkot – we came close and might have got over the line had we timed our declaration right. I had one of my best games for England, winning the Man of the Match award. After Cooky had won the toss I joined Rooty at 102 for 3 and we put on 179. Both of us made hundreds and while Rooty was watchful – he did not reverse sweep until after he had reached his hundred – I played my shots right from the beginning. It was a good batting wicket and I enjoyed my duels with Ashwin and Jadeja, two very different spinners. Ashwin, a fantastic bowler, has got more craft and skill than his spinning partner, but Jadeja bowls the fastest left-arm spinners I have ever faced. At the end of the first day's play I was 99 but did not lose any sleep over getting my hundred and the next morning hit three fours in four balls off Umesh Yadav, their opening bowler, before falling for 117. With Stokesy also making a hundred we got to 537. But it was the events of the final day that made this Test the great 'what if' of this tour.

We had a lead of 309 and on the final day were 260 for 3 when Cooky declared, giving us a minimum of 49 overs to scare India or even win. With hindsight if we had declared a bit earlier we would probably have won that game. We had them six down. Kohli was the only guy who resisted us. Cooky might have judged the declaration better had he not been batting. He scored a hundred, becoming the first Englishman to score

1,000 Test runs in India and it is possible he was thinking more of that than when to declare.

The lesson India took from Rajkot was there should be no grass on the pitch. On the previous tour Dhoni had his clashes with Indian groundsmen but England still won. But in the Kohli reign it was different. The wickets were not vicious turners as Indian wickets can be. They were quite flat; really good wickets. The ball came down a little bit slower but to put it very simply in the next four Tests after Rajkot their batters scored a lot more runs than ours and their bowlers bowled better than ours. And at crucial moments England dropped catches. In the second Test at Visakhapatnam Kohli, on 56, top-edged Stokesy and Rash at fine leg floored him. He went on to make 167, India reached 455 and after that we were always struggling.

I had so far in my three-year England career batted in various positions. At Mohali, where I loved the biryani, I had two more new batting positions. I started the Test at number four, the first time I was so high in the order. Then in the second innings I came in at number three after poor Haseeb Hameed, the young Lancastrian who had made a brilliant Test debut at Rajkot, broke his left little finger. This meant that since my debut in 2014 I had filled every slot in England's batting line-up from number one to number nine. It illustrated the shake-up taking place in our cricket. India, well settled under Kohli, had no such problems. We were always behind and lost easily.

We then had a short break in Dubai. I took the opportunity to go to Mecca, which always energizes me, before returning to Mumbai for the fourth Test. For the first time in nearly decades there was no Tendulkar playing in his home ground although the crowd occasionally sang, 'Sachin, Sachin' and some even wore Tendulkar T-shirts. The Wankhede Stadium has a lovely setting with the Arabian Sea in the background. When Cooky won the toss and batted I did not expect to be walking out in mid-afternoon. Cooky had another new batting partner, Keaton Jennings. He had a bit of luck, being dropped before he had scored, and I joined him at 136 for 2. I was impressed with the way he cut and pulled and we put on 94, taking England to 230 for 2. I had made 50 when I was bowled trying to slog-sweep Ashwin. Jennings scored a century on debut, as Cooky had done a decade earlier. Cooky's had been in Nagpur, the city famous for oranges, Jennings's was in the city of Tendulkar. We should have made more than 400 and this was underlined when Kohli made 235 and we were beaten by an innings.

The last Test at Chennai also saw another innings defeat yet it had begun so well. I really enjoyed the wicket. Now established at number four, I came in with the score on 21 for 2. Both Cooky and Keaton were out but Rooty was playing well. India had recalled the legspinner Amit Mishra but I had no worries about hitting him against the turn and on the up. We put on 146 before Rooty fell on 88. Mishra was bowling when I reached my hundred, getting to 99 with an inside-out drive, which can be so satisfying, and then a tap for a single, my fourth century of the year for England. I ended the first day 120 not out, we were

284 for 4, and set for what looked like a big score. The second morning I hit Ashwin for a huge six but then top-edged Yadav on 146. We ended up with 477 which should have made us safe but India responded with a monumental 759, Karun Nair making an unbeaten 303 and Lokesh Rahul 199. Our second innings was poor. I made 44, falling to a great catch by Ashwin at mid-on, and we lost by an innings for the second successive Test.

The defeats were devastating but I came away with wonderful memories of India. Indian cricket, which is so rich, was using the money it brings from television and sponsorship to expand the game. Two of the Tests, Rajkot in the west and Visakhapatnam in the south, were new Test centres – part of a policy of taking high-level cricket around that vast country – and I struck up a wonderful rapport with the Indian crowd. The last time I had played India was in Birmingham and the Indian crowd had booed me. Here there was none of that, the fans could not have more friendly and welcoming and while I had played in India before, playing Test cricket in front of such crowds and in stadiums with wonderful facilities was an amazing experience. I also began to realize why Indian cricketers say that when they are at home they cannot often venture out, such is their status in that country. Cricket is on a different level over there. It has been said it is like a religion and that is right. It is everywhere. You drive into town from the airport and go past billboards where cricketers are advertising products. In your hotel you get into a lift and there are pictures of the whole team in the lift staring back at you as you climb the floors. The newspapers run huge articles about the visiting players, some of whom are used to promote products – Brett Lee has fronted many Indian advertising campaigns. People not only wanted autographs all the time but we were mobbed so often that at times we couldn't even leave the hotel. I don't know how the Indian guys cope. We stayed in our rooms a lot and the team room with table tennis was very popular with many of us playing *FIFA*. The result was during the tour as a team we got a lot closer and tighter but, having said that, sometimes it would have been nice if we could have gone out. The room service at hotels was very good but I did sorely miss going to Nando's.

CHAPTER 14

GLORIOUS SUMMER TURNS DARK WINTER

could not have wished for a better summer than the one I had in 2017. If the Oval was one of those magical moments that will never again be repeated – a first Test hat-trick, like a first Test century, is always very special – I had many more moments to savour. We showed in the final Test at Old Trafford that England does not always go from boom to bust. On winning the toss we were always in command and I took centre stage in the second innings. Though we had a first-innings lead of 136, the South Africans refused to lie down, and had even begun to sense victory – we were 153 for 7, 289 ahead. I had batted number nine in the first innings after Rojo but now came in ahead of him, the sort of tinkering with my position I was all too familiar with. I had an escape when dropped on 15 off Keshav Maharaj in the slips but I knew we needed runs, we couldn't sit back and wait for things to happen. In 66 balls I hit 75 not out with Rojo, who made 11, Broady and Jimmy all giving me valuable support. The moment that gave me the most amusement was when one of my three sixes sailed into our dressing room and Bluey took the catch, then stood and held up the ball like a fisherman with a prize salmon. South Africa would have to make

380 to draw the series. They never looked like winning but at 163 for 3, and with Amla and du Plessis going well, it was possible they could prevent us winning.

I was very confident I could turn the tide, so Rooty let me have a silly point and a short-leg. I bowled Amla an off-break, he came down, was hit on the pads and I was certain he was lbw. The review proved me right. I decided to flight one to Quinton de Kock who edged to Cooky, and then Theunis de Bruyn edged to Stokesy. In eleven balls I had taken three for five. Morkel decided to slog me but it landed in Rooty's hands at mid-off and the next ball, the fifth ball of my nineteenth over, Duanne Olivier pushed forward and Stokesy did the rest at slip. I could not thank him enough. He had taken eight catches off my bowling in the series. I had got a five-fer, 5 for 69, 25 wickets in the series, five more than Jimmy although his average at 14 apiece was better than mine at 15 apiece. It gave me another Man of the Match award, my fifth since my debut in 2014, matching that of Rooty. Yet before the Oval many had seen me as England's second-choice spinner after Liam Dawson.

Against the West Indies, who followed South Africa, my best performance was in the second Test, which we lost, though I made 84 in the second innings, the highest score in our second knock. But wonderful batting by Shai Hope and Kraigg Brathwaite saw them home. I did though have Brathwaite caught by Stokesy at slip when he was 95. But we had won the first Test at Edgbaston by an innings, and went on to win the third at Lord's by nine wickets to take the series 2-1.

All this was a prelude to the innings that gave me the most joy and led to our proud victory in the five-match ODI series. 24 September 2017 was such a special day for me. That was when we played the third Royal London ODI against the West Indies at Bristol. Put into bat, I came in number eight, when Rooty got out and the score was 217 for 6 after 35 overs. We had been 206 for 3 at one stage when a score in excess of 400 looked very likely. Now it was a stretch to think we could even get to much more than 250. I started sedately and got to 39 playing a few strokes but not lofting the ball much. Then I decided I must find the leg-side boundary; in fourteen balls I moved from 39 to 100, hitting eight sixes, most of them on the leg-side. When I got to my century I raised my bat and pointed in the direction of where I knew Walee was sitting. Our 369 was always going to be a tall order for the West Indies and we won by 124 runs. As I collected my Man of the Match award I felt I now truly belonged to England. I told Walee that later and he said, 'You are right, Bro.'

I spent the weeks before we left for Australia preparing for the Ashes certain that nobody could deny my status as an England cricketer. On a previous Ashes tour the team had been taken to Austria. But this time the feeling was we were already tight as a group and there was not a lot of need for that of sort of bonding exercise. We had a camp up in Loughborough for a couple of days but we didn't do anything major as a team which, given how busy our summer had been, was a very sensible decision.

I did not have to be told that my first Ashes series in Australia would be a challenge and I worked hard at getting fitter and making sure I was in good condition to last the whole tour. There was a lot of running, gym work, working on my core muscles. I also worked hard in the nets. I would get up each morning at about six, say my prayers, then pick up Kadeer and Omar and head for the indoor nets at Edgbaston, getting there by 7.30 or 8. I worked there for two to three hours on my batting and my bowling. I used the bowling machine with Kadeer and Omar throwing balls at me, over the wicket, round the wicket. I worked on different scenarios, playing the ball, leaving it and coping with short-pitched bowling. I wanted to make sure I got everything covered when facing the fast bowlers, when to leave the ball, when to hook the short ball. As I played the faster deliveries I thought of all the Australian pace bowlers coming at me – Starc, Hazlewood, whoever. I was facing real pace in the nets and making sure I coped with the bounce. In order to generate pace we tried a hardish rubber ball, red in colour. We dumped the ball in a bucket of water which gave it extreme pace and we also wet the mat. I have never worked so hard playing pace as I did in the Edgbaston nets before the Ashes tour began. I wasn't worried about spin at all; I had played Lyon before in England, I played in India against Ashwin and Jadeja, the home of spin, and scored two hundreds.

Just before I flew out I also pledged myself to Worcestershire. There had been some turmoil in the county and Bumpy had left but I saw no reason to change. Warwickshire were keen to lure me back and Dad would have quite liked me to return. But I told him Worcestershire had supported and encouraged me when I needed it most and I saw no reason to turn my back on them. So I arrived in Australia feeling good about my preparations and ready to take on the Aussies. Little did I know the problems I would face, even before we had played a match.

On the first day at Perth after I had batted and bowled we got down for fielding practice, and I was just throwing the ball when I pulled my side. It was only a slight pull but I could feel there was something. I missed the two practice games at Perth and Adelaide, more as a precaution, just to make sure nothing major happened. I played the third practice game at Townsville, in northern Queensland, to get some overs under my belt and be on the field for my legs. I didn't score many runs, I came in with the score at 419 for 5 when we were looking to declare, but I bowled a total of 48 overs in the two innings, performing quite decently on a really flat wicket.

I was pretty confident going into the Test matches given the summer I'd had. In the run up to the series there had been a lot of noise from the Australian players about how they would end careers. Smith and Lyon were particularly vociferous. These were silly comments. I blanked them out. It was typical of Australia, a team that nobody likes. Every team, every player dislikes Australia because of the way they behave on the field and how arrogantly they come across. As I have said during the 2015 Ashes they were in our face and we won that. So such silly talk by the Australians did not worry me or the team as we went into the first Test at Brisbane.

We batted first and I was batting six. When Lyon came on to bowl I felt really good facing him. I went out determined to hit him and slogged the fourth ball he bowled to me for six. He did get me out lbw for 38 which I saw as one of those things that can happen. It didn't worry me. I felt pretty good, I felt I'd played him quite well, quite aggressively and that is how I wanted to play.

My first problem was when I came on to bowl. Rooty brought me on first change, it was still a new ball, the seam was hard. I was bowling to Usman Khawaja, their number three batsman. In my third over I turned one sharply away from him. But the next one while bowled identically went straight and he was lbw. But as soon as I got Khawaja out I ripped my index finger with the seam of the new ball and immediately realized it was going to be a difficult problem for me. I had done this four or five years before. It was hard for me to grip the ball. I couldn't even put my finger onto the ball. The more balls I was bowling the worse my finger was getting. I was really worried and as I continued bowling blood started to pour out of the finger. I had to go off and glue my finger back together. So now there was glue all over my finger, glue between my grip and my fingers all to make sure I could wrap it up and try and bowl somehow. Even just touching the ball with my finger was painful, let alone gripping it. I took painkillers and kept taping the finger. I carried on bowling but it was affecting me and I couldn't really concentrate. It got so bad I was just trying to make sure I could land the ball at least half way down the pitch. I did get another wicket, Hazlewood, and in the end bowled 30 overs but finally I had to tell Rooty, 'I can't put my finger on the ball right now.' I also bowled in the Australian second innings but I struggled to grip the ball. I bowled only 4 overs in that innings. I just could not carry on with my finger so sensitive. I was in great pain for the whole Test.

The finger did not affect my ability to bat but there was a psychological impact. When something's not quite right it affects your entire game, even your batting. I was going out to bat feeling depressed about my inability to bowl well because of my finger. For me the crucial moment of the series came when I was batting in the second innings. I was given out stumped. It was a very controversial moment. It was based on how thick the line was. The line at the end where I was batting actually gets thicker. Part of the line was normal and then the line bent a little and then curved back in. After an extremely granular inspection of replays the verdict was that I was out. If I was bowling I would have expected the umpire to give a decision in my favour. That was definitely a critical moment for me in the series. Until the stumping I was playing really well and confidently and I had made a good 40. Even though Lyon was bowling excellently I felt we had been a little bit negative against him, and in that innings I was trying to make sure we did not allow him to dictate to us. Had the stumping not been given who is to say what would have happened? Perhaps if I had got a score there the whole series could have been different.

After that decision I did begin to think for the first time since I had faced him almost two years earlier, oh, Lyon's got me out twice now.

The next Test was the day-night match in Adelaide, it was a pink ball Test match and my finger had not really healed but despite that I was playing. I had to play. We had to try and win. In that Test, despite my finger being really sore, I bowled a total of 29 overs, 24 in the first innings. Batting number six, I was decent in the first innings, made 25, and again got out to Nathan Lyon, a spectacular one-handed diving catch. All credit to him but on another day he might not have got anywhere near the ball. He also got me in the second innings as well. I struggled with my finger when bowling but I managed to get through that game. So after a second comprehensive defeat we were already looking at a 2-0 deficit. Thankfully there was a break after that game and my finger started to heal, but I felt that I had lost a lot of confidence, one because of our being behind in the series, and two because I hadn't done anything yet.

It was after the second Test that I started to obsess about Lyon, a bowler I had never before seen as a threat. Now I brooded about him a bit too much and I think that was when I stepped on the down escalator. From there my series kept going downhill. I found it difficult with people saying I should be dropped. Having had a great summer, after just two games I was under pressure again to hold on to my place. Then with Nathan Lyon bowling fantastically well, getting a lot of wickets, consistently getting me, there was even more pressure on me.

This was a big series, and the noise was everywhere. For the first time in my whole career I let the media get to me.

In the third Test at Perth I had yet another batting position. I had batted at six in the first two Tests. Because we were getting rolled, with our last five wickets going for thirty or forty runs, the management felt Bluey was getting wasted so they put him in at number six and me at seven. Before the Test Rooty told me, 'It's not because of the way you're batting, it's just that Nathan Lyon is bowling so well and he has got left-hander, left-hander, left-hander, and we want to split that up slightly.' Of course throughout my Test career I had been moved about in the order, so I was used to it. But given what was happening it only added to my declining confidence. However, you could say it worked as Bluey got 119, while Australia rumbled on towards the Ashes with another crushing win.

Before the fourth Test it did go through my mind that I should try to change things. I asked Ramps and Collingwood and others for ideas. I normally take a middle-and-leg guard. I said, 'I'm thinking about going maybe middle-stump to try and cover the ball.' Their response was, 'It's not a bad plan.' So I took middle-stump guard, tried to move over more to the off-side and cover the ball a bit more. I tried that in the nets. But actually, I should have gone the other way. I should have gone leg-stump, showing Lyon my wickets and then played him through the off-side.

By the time we came to Melbourne for the fourth Test I began to feel I was probably going to be dropped soon. I decided this would be my last game on tour and I was just going to go out and try and play my shots. I told myself, 'I'm just going to go out and be very aggressive and try and take Lyon down. I've had enough of just prodding.' I hit Lyon's first ball for six and got after him a little bit. Then I went to play a shot over extra cover and I hit the back of my leg and the buckle of my pad ripped off. Half the pad was hanging off my left leg. I called for a new pad, but I said, 'Give it to me later.' Normally I would have changed the pads straightaway. But I was in such a state of mind, playing my shots and rushing things in my mind, I thought, you know what, I'll just change them after the over. I batted with a broken buckle on my left pad. Lyon then bowled me the worst ball he bowled at me in the series and I smashed it straight to cover. But as I walked off I was thinking, at least I played the way I wanted to play, and I wasn't just plodding around and being indecisive.

The media criticism I faced after this felt very harsh. I always feel, as soon as I have a couple of bad games, it's like, 'Oh, this guy can't be in the team.' I remember at Lord's after I got out to India they said, 'Oh, he can't play the short ball' and now it was 'Yeah, he can't play spin.' Throughout your career you are going to have these little hiccups in your cricket but in my case the critics converted my failures into an existential thing, asking how could I possibly be an England player. What made things even more difficult was the harder I was trying – I actually tried really hard in the nets – the worse it got and the chorus against me got louder. I spoke to Rooty and he was very reassuring. He told me not to worry. In fact all the players were very supportive.

However, that was not the case with everyone in the coaching staff and the management team.

Soon after the Melbourne match Paul Collingwood, who had just joined the England coaching staff, told the media, 'You can see a muddled mind.' I was shocked to hear that. To make such a statement without any warning felt unfair. After the game, as we were travelling to Sydney for the fifth Test and were sitting in the airport lounge, Colly came up and told me, 'We need to have a chat.' Then he repeated what he had voiced publicly saying, 'Look, I thought you were muddled.' I explained to him that actually my innings at Melbourne was the one time in the series I was really clear. I knew exactly how I wanted to go about things. I said I was disappointed that he made that statement without discussing it with me first and that I found that difficult. He indicated that he understood my feelings.

The thing is I've played like that in the past and when it comes off everyone is like, 'Oh, what a brave innings', or 'You know, he's taken the game away.' I know that because of the way I play. If it doesn't come off I will get criticized.

What also hurt me was the way ex-England players in the commentary box went for me. Graeme Swann, Michael Vaughan and Geoffrey Boycott were very critical. Probably not Swanny so much, but Vaughan and Boycott especially have, I feel, always been very against me being in the England side. For whatever reason, they don't want me there. They don't think I am good enough. They don't think I belong. So, when I'm doing well their praise is very grudging: it's 'Oh yeah, he's doing okay'; never 'Oh yeah, he's doing really well.' And when I'm doing badly it's 'He can't be in the team any more.' Boycott has said his mother could play me and I think it's quite disrespectful to get your mother involved. I think they do it to grab attention, and generate a bit of controversy.

As for Swanny saying he would have loved to work with me on my bowling, that quite mystifies me. I would see him every morning at the ground and he wouldn't say a word to me about my bowling. Never once did he come up to me, or have a word with me, about what he thought of my bowling. If someone is struggling then surely you can go up to him and as a former England spinner offer your help. In any case, as Swanny knows, visiting spinners do not do well in Australia. Ashwin hasn't done that well. Nor did Yasir Shah. It is a difficult place to go and bowl, and Steve Smith was on such good form; he was really hard to bowl at.

In the past I have let the criticism wash over me. Now there was so much of it on social media, it was impossible to ignore and for the first time in my career I let it get to me a bit. I had to keep reassuring myself that actually it doesn't mean that I had suddenly, a little over five months after the Oval and three months after Bristol, become a bad player; I'd just had a bad series. But the criticism got me so down I wanted the tour to be over. When we got to Sydney I didn't think I was going to play. Rooty came up to me and said, 'Mo, I want a word with you.' He went on, 'I know there's been a lot of talk that you're not going to play but you're playing.' I found that very uplifting because it meant that the media had got it wrong. They said I played because Woakesy got injured. That was not the case. I was always playing.

That last Test in Sydney was a difficult Test match for us as well. We got smashed in Sydney. But once it was over I was pretty glad the whole series was over, even with that 4-0 defeat in the record books. The one-day series came and we won pretty convincingly. I bowled quite well in all of them. The difference between our red-ball and white-ball cricket was the way Morgy had got the side together. The one-day team was so much more relaxed. The atmosphere around the changing room is different to the Test team, more laidback. Test cricket is a lot more intense. The one-day stuff is much more fun. There are younger guys, different personalities. The one-day guys are almost like a separate team. Morgy has had a big part to play in that, the way he carried his form and the way he captains the side. Rooty has just come into the Test side as a captain and he is obviously going to take a bit of time to establish his own style in that role. Our performance in white-ball cricket was some solace in what had been a grim winter and showed how we can turn things round.

Interestingly, I didn't find the Australian press bad. The English press was much worse. What was strange was the Australian crowd. I had been told how keen the Australians were on the Ashes. I expected the grounds to be full of Aussie supporters. It surprised me how few turned up for the Tests despite the fact that they were winning: perhaps because the matches weren't that close. There were so many empty seats. If it wasn't for the Barmy Army, a lot of the time you could have heard a pin drop. But despite the fact that not many Australians turned up to watch us, they were ready to abuse the England players and some of the abuse I received was racial. I heard comments directed at me like 'When is your kebab shop opening?' I would turn round to see who had said it and find guys were sticking their fingers up at me. I expected Australia to be quite rough, but not as bad as this. I hadn't heard such comments for a long time. I got some of this abuse even in the practice games and it made me think how different it was in India. As soon as you turn up there the crowds would stand up and they would cheer you. They love their cricketers but they do not denigrate the opposition. Australians have a lot to learn from the Indians. And from us in England.

The absence of Ben Stokes – he'd been left out after being charged with affray after an incident outside a nightclub – had a massive impact on the series. The conditions in Australia would have been perfect for him. He had been unbelievable in South Africa. He would have thrived against Australia; there is his bowling, which on those wickets would have generated pace that would have worried the Australian batsmen, and then there is his character. The Australians would have been intimidated by his sheer presence, and a bit scared of him as a player.

We missed him in the changing room because he's the one guy who if things are down can really pick you up and provide the lead. Rooty captained brilliantly, he's tactically very good, but Stokesy has been our best player probably for the last year or so and brings to the dressing room a personality and a capacity to lift the side in a way that nobody else can.

I understood why the ECB felt unable to have him on the Ashes tour after the negative publicity and I realize it was a difficult decision to drop him from the tour party. We spoke quite a bit about Stokesy being excluded. He was playing in New Zealand at the time and we felt if he was playing over there he could be playing for us. It was frustrating, but the governing body had to make a tough call. Stokesy is our best player, we needed him as we were struggling and to have had him in Australia would have helped us, I have no doubt about that.

Stokesy's absence meant the atmosphere wasn't the same as it had been in recent series, particularly in South Africa the previous winter and in the summer. Stokesy is somebody I'm quite close with. I missed him a lot at times. He was replaced by Steven Finn who then got injured during practice at Perth at the start of the tour. So Tom Curran was sent for as replacement for Finny, and he is a young kid from Surrey who'd been in and out of the team that summer, so I knew him and that changed things. Not that we didn't stick together, as we were still a tight unit, but in general the atmosphere wasn't great. I think deep down maybe everybody knew that we were going to struggle on this trip. The one plus was that while in India I had missed

Nando's and here I ate there a lot because fortunately everything's Halal in Australia.

I know some people felt Australia did a bit of reverse bodyline with the use of the short ball, particularly against our lower-order batsmen. As I see it, it is in the rules. If you feel a player's not capable of handling the ball very well and if you have guys that bowl at 90 miles per hour then you are entitled to make life uncomfortable for nine, ten, jack. When the ball's not doing much and you've got pace in your team then that is one tactic that you probably have to use.

My big support came from my family. They came out for the last three Test matches. I spoke to my dad often. He kept saying just keep trying. My brothers said you've played for England for a while now, just enjoy yourself.

In New Zealand in the first Test I went into bat not expecting the score to be 18 for 5 in the eleventh over. The ball was swinging and it was a pink-ball game. It was the first time we had played with the pink ball against the white screen and it was difficult to pick up the ball when it was really full. But they bowled fantastically well. We just managed to nick and miss everything. These guys have done that to other teams and that can happen. We did it to Australia in 2015. Yes, we did get stuck on the crease and obviously we didn't play well. I think that had to be the effect of the Australia series, a lot of players naturally feeling under pressure, having had a bad winter. We were bowled out for 58, there was no going back and we lost by an innings.

Then the day before the second Test at Christchurch Rooty pulled me to one side of the field as we were warming up and told me, 'We are going to go with Jack [Leach] as the spinner.' I said, 'First of all I appreciate that you gave me a long run. I could have been dropped a couple of games ago. I'm sorry I didn't perform and I will try my best to get back into this team – I'll work even harder as I'm still hungry to play for England.' You are always disappointed when you're not playing, but to be honest it was a bit of a relief. I felt I needed a break. I had to get away from the spotlight a little bit. I was never going to walk away after the Ashes. I know in the past players have walked away after a couple of bad games feeling under pressure. Graeme Swann did that on the previous Ashes tour there. I was never going to do that. I was going to stick around with the team and do the best I could. Give my 100 per cent still. I have always done that when playing this great game. I am not going to change now. To play for England is the greatest prize you can have in cricket and I shall not give up on that.

CHAPTER 15

BACK ON HOME SOIL

While it was a blow to lose my spot in the Test side in New Zealand, a very good distraction came along at just the right time: my first season in the Indian Premier League.

When I put my name forward to play IPL, I wasn't too bothered if I didn't get picked but I was curious to learn about the process. The England team were travelling together in Perth, winding up the ODI series, when the IPL auction took place. A few of the guys were very anxious and because we were all together it was even more tense. I put my headphones on because I didn't want to hear all the chat about it. Morgy tapped me on the shoulder and said, 'You've been bid on.' He showed me on his phone that Chennai and Royal Challengers Bangalore were bidding for me. When I ended up with RCB I was over the moon – particularly because Woakesy was going there too. And the rest of the line-up was incredible: to play alongside, instead of against, people like Virat Kohli, AB de Villiers, Brendon McCullum and Quinton de Kock was an amazing experience. I didn't end up playing as many games as I would have liked – I sat on the bench for the first nine matches – but it was a real thrill to walk out in the RCB kit for my first game in Hyderabad. My performances weren't anything special and in a blink the whole experience seemed to be over but now that I've got a taste, I definitely want to go back. The way the whole thing is run is fantastic, and I've never heard crowds supporting players so loudly before. RCB have an amazing following, and the standard of cricket is extremely high. If you look at the players coming through in India, their skill-set is incredible and I think the creation of the IPL has definitely taken the game forward.

Sitting out the England vs Pakistan Test series in May 2018 was no bad thing from my perspective: after Australia, New Zealand and India, it was great to be home and spending some family time with Firuza and Abu Bakr. Now four years old, he's very active and loves cricket and football nearly as much as I do. We love watching Liverpool together and whenever I'm playing for England on home soil, Firuza brings him along to watch. He ends up singing Barmy Army chants around the house for days after each game.

While I was enjoying time at home in Birmingham, with the occasional outing for Worcestershire, I was making sure I stayed as fit as possible as Australia were coming back to England in June for a five-match ODI series. It was to be a very different Australian side than the team we met just months before in the Ashes as in March Steve Smith and David Warner were banned from representing Australia at cricket for twelve months following a ball-tampering incident in South Africa. The fact that the Australians were actively tampering with the ball didn't surprise me at all – we'd thought that during the Ashes there might have been something of that order going on but we had no proof of it, so of course you give the opposition the benefit of the doubt. What surprised me was that it was front-page news and became such a big talking point – a sad example of cricket getting headlines for the worst reasons.

Even though I'd missed the Tests against Pakistan, I was starting to feel confident about my form again and in early June, playing for Worcestershire against my former team Warwickshire in a Royal London Cup game, I scored 114 runs from 75 balls. The fluency I'd struggled to find over the winter had returned, and I was looking forward to playing for England again. It's now over ten years since I signed with Worcestershire, which I still think is one of the best decisions I ever made, and it was an honour in late 2017 to extend my contract with them until 2022. The dressing room, from the days of Graeme Hick and Vik to the current line-up, has always been a supportive, kind atmosphere and Worcestershire has really moulded me as a player. It will be an honour to see out my cricket career with them.

It was Ramadan and I felt like I was seeing the ball really well again. My teammates are always amazed at my routine during Ramadan – during the holy month, I get up at 2 or 2.30 in the morning and eat something light, often a piece of toast, two dates and some water, and then I won't break the fast until night time, with no liquids passing my mouth all day until the main meal at about 9.45 pm. The main reason we fast is to appreciate what we have, and to get to know the hunger that less fortunate people feel every day. And as the fasting goes on you eat less and less, your stomach shrinks and you realize that sometimes you eat too much. I find it sharpens my concentration. And it's an extra incentive to keep batting: you know that if you get out you've got to go back to the changing room where there's food everywhere. When I'm fasting it really helps to be doing something.

Before we played Australia, though, we had a warm-up game against Scotland in Edinburgh which proved trickier than anticipated. It looked like we had it in the bag but we ended up losing by six runs. It really put the press on our backs. The usual cricket experts were saying that we think we're too good now at the short-form of the game and that Australia was going to beat us. We were pretty confident the Scotland result was just a blip and it was only ever meant to be a warm-up game. We definitely shouldn't have lost that match but the strength of the team is shown in the way we moved on quickly as a group.

The first game of the Australia series, at the Oval on June 13, began with our opponents lining up and shaking all of our hands – Tim Paine had suggested it to Morgy and I thought it was a good idea, to try to draw a line under the unpleasantness that has characterized the recent Australian teams. I understood what they were trying to do but things don't change so quickly. All the teams around the world hate Australia and it's a shame really. Yes, they play tough cricket and they've been fantastic performers for years and years but I always say I'd rather be a cricketer who's average but known for being a decent guy than be an absolute legend who no one's got a good word to say about.

We bowled first and I made an impact with the ball straight away, getting three key wickets – Finch, Marsh and Paine – pretty quickly. Rash got two wickets as well which was great as the plan we'd been working on for ages – to come on together, bowling in tandem and change the momentum of the game – was suddenly very visibly working. While Australia's total of 214 should have been an easier target than it ended up being, I was the Man of the Match, and the media started calling us the spin twins. It's very important for a player to make an impression early in the series, as that takes some of the pressure off and lets you get on with your game for the later matches.

The third ODI at Trent Bridge was a match I'll remember forever. We batted first and Bluey and Alex Hales were in the form of their lives. Every ball was like watching a highlights reel. The batters were electric. Bluey played superbly to get to 139 and when he was out, we were 310 for 2, with more than 15 overs to go. It was clear our score was going to be massive but it was incredible to get a world record score of 481. I came to the crease in the forty-eighth over at 459 for 4, and after Morgy went next ball I faced Jhye Richardson, who was on a hat-trick. I survived to make a handful of runs before I got run out trying to get a bye off the keeper – even though we ended up with an innings of 481 I wanted it to be 482. To give credit to the Aussies, they really did put the brakes on in the last 4 overs – we'd thought for a moment that 500 runs might be possible.

The fifth ODI at Old Trafford may have seemed stressful for spectators, as Jos Buttler, in the form of his life, rapidly ran out of batting partners chasing Australia's modest total of 205. We desperately wanted to sweep the series 5-0 and Jos was clearly incredibly hungry. When you're winning you win games like that and when you're losing you lose games like that. I think it was actually worse for Australia, who had a hope of winning the game and got really excited and pumped up, and then all of a sudden lost. It would have been heartbreaking for them.

Across the five-match series Rash and I ended up the joint highest wicket takers, the most wickets ever taken by spinners in an ODI series of that length. I got a little criticism as a batsman for giving my wicket away too cheaply, but actually since the other batters are in such incredible form and I'm coming in at six or seven, I have to turn up and play shots. I'm not the sort of guy who's going to think about my average or getting a not out – I'm always trying to do what's best for the team. I'm not somebody who's going to look back on their stats some day and bemoan my average – every time I play a bad shot or even a silly shot, at the time I'm thinking that's what's best for the team.

Beating Australia six games in a row (including the T20) was fantastic. It felt like a continuation of the work we did to win the ODI series in Australia after the Ashes, where even with their best side at full strength we beat them convincingly 4-1. Without wanting to sound boastful it was great to personally do quite well and send them back without winning a game. I do feel for Australia to a certain extent – it's the only time I'll feel sorry for them at all because they ran into our batters at the wrong time, when they were at their absolute peak. Because they weren't winning any games they had to be humble, which doesn't come easily to them. After the series they did come into our dressing room for a friendly chat, which made a change from the poisonous atmosphere of the Ashes – they're good guys, particularly when you get them on their own but when you're playing against them, especially when they're doing well, they're all over you and very aggressive. I'm the sort of guy that plays to win but at the same time I'm fundamentally relaxed – at the end of the day it's just a game of cricket. It's going to take Australia some time to rebuild. But at least with Justin Langer in charge now the team culture is more important than the individual. People respect him and I think only good things can come from his appointment.

And winning the series underscored for me that I think that right now is the very best time to be playing for England. While I can see that Kabir and Vik Solanki struggled to fit into the England teams of their playing prime, people like Morgy, Alastair Cook and Trevor Bayliss have made the dressing room of today incredibly welcoming. There's always been an element of English cricketers coming from posh schools and being a closed club, but now it's more normal to have teams made up from people of different backgrounds and I'm sure the side is stronger for it.

When I look back on my life and career, my overwhelming feeling is gratitude. First and foremost I'm grateful to God for where I am today in terms of my health, my family and the blessings I have. It might sound silly but I'm incredibly thankful for everything I can do with ease, from playing sport to really basic things like going to the toilet.

I also owe huge thanks to my parents for supporting me all the time. While my father has been very present in these pages, my mother is the special one in my heart and a huge influence on my life. She said to me once years ago, when I first started to let my beard grow and try to act like a Muslim, that I was the coolness of her eyes, which is an expression from the Koran – when your eyes become cool, that means you have peace and tranquillity and joy. I was really touched by that, and I could see that I made her happy. People think I represent England and I represent Islam, but more important to me is that I represent my parents and I always want to make them proud of me.

And my wife Firuza who has sacrificed so much for my career. She goes to so many weddings and social engagements on her own because I'm not here and I know that mentally and emotionally that can be tough. My brothers and my sister also always support me no matter what. My brilliant sister Azba has had it particularly tough because she was the only girl in the family for a very long time and all we talked about was cricket – she's managed to forge her own path in a really impressive way and I'm so proud of her.

I'm also thankful for my extended family, as well as the people who pray for me and all my supporters. It's not praise I want from them, it's prayers, and not just for cricket but for life in general. I'm an incredibly lucky guy.